Words of Life

Jesus and the Promise of the Ten Commandments Today

Adam Hamilton

Bestselling Author of *Making Sense of the Bible*

Words of Life
Jesus and the Promise of the Ten Commandments Today
Children's Leader Guide

978-1-7910-1335-6

20 21 22 23 24 25 26 27 28 29 — 10 9 8 7 6 5 4 3 2 1
MANUFACTURED IN THE UNITED STATES OF AMERICA

Contents

Introduction

This children's leader guide is designed for use with Adam Hamilton's book *Words of Life: Jesus and the Promise of the Ten Commandments Today*. This guide includes ten lessons, one for each of the commandments. Feel free to use this guide with one lesson per week. Or, if you wish to complete the study in fewer weeks, one of these shorter lesson plans may be suitable:

5-week study: two commandments each week

6-week study: Commandments 1 and 2, Commandments 3 and 4, Commandment 5, Commandments 6 and 7, Commandments 8 and 9, Commandment 10

The lessons in this guide, designed for children in kindergarten through the sixth grade, are presented in a large group/small group format. Children begin with time spent at activity centers, followed by time together as a large group. Next, children will move into age-specific groups, followed by closing worship to end the session. Each lesson plan contains the following sections:

Focus for the Teacher

The information in this section will provide you with background information about the week's lesson. Use this section as a devotional as you prepare to lead the session.

Explore Interest Groups

This section provides activities that invite children to explore the theme for the day. These activities offer an introduction to the commandment of the day. You may choose to offer all of the activities for children to choose from or pick your favorite based on your group's specific needs.

Large Group

The large group time introduces the Scripture for the day. Each focus Bible verse will be one of the Ten Commandments. The Bible story for the day will sometimes, but not always, be a Scripture text that illuminates the commandment.

Children will engage with each of the Ten Commandments through hands-on activities, ritual, and prayer. Each week, your group will add to a mobile displaying each of the Ten Commandments. Each week you will be encouraged to return to the mobile as a way of tracking your learning and seeing the commandments as guidelines for living a balanced life. Large group time will also include learning a memory verse. Encourage the children to practice their Bible skills by helping the children find Scripture references in the Bible even if the activity does not require reading directly from the Bible.

Small Groups

Small groups offer age-specific opportunities to explore the commandment of the day. It is recommended that each small group contain no more than ten children. You may need to have more than one group for each age level.

Younger Children

The activities in this section are designed for children in grades K–2.

Older Children

The activities in this section are designed for children in grades 3–6.

Closing Worship

Closing worship time will bring the groups back together for a review of the lesson. This time will be spent revisiting the commandment of the day and applying it to their lives. Groups will finish by praying together.

Reproducible Pages

At the end of each lesson are reproducible pages, to be photocopied and handed out for all the children to use during that lesson's activities.

Supplies

Specialized supplies are listed with each activity, but not at the beginning of the session. Standard supplies are assumed to be plain paper, construction paper, pencils, crayons, markers, scissors, tape, and glue.

Schedule

Many churches have weeknight programs that include an evening meal; an intergenerational gathering time; and classes for children, youth, and adults. The following schedule illustrates one way to organize a weeknight program.

Weeknight

5:00	Meal
6:00	Intergenerational gathering introducing weekly themes and places for the lesson. This time may include presentations, skits, music, and opening or closing prayers.
6:15–7:15	Classes for children, youth, and adults.

Churches may want to do this study as a Sunday school program. This setting would be similar to the weeknight setting. The following schedule takes into account a shorter class time, which is the norm for Sunday morning programs.

Sunday

10 minutes	Intergenerational gathering
45 minutes	Classes for children, youth, and adults

Choose a schedule that works best for your congregation and its existing Christian education programs.

Adam Hamilton writes that he believes "God longs for . . . these commandments [to] be inscribed on our *hearts*, understood with our minds, and lived in our daily lives," citing Jeremiah 31. This is the focus of the children's programming: to provide a space where the children can encounter the commandments as relevant guidelines that show them how to live. As you teach, know that you have what it takes to guide the children through learning one of the foundations of faithful living. Approach each lesson with an open mind, open heart, and careful preparation. God will do the rest.

May your fellowship be blessed as you seek to share God's guidelines for living well with the children in your care.

1. At the Center of It All

Objectives

The children will:

- encounter the story of the Ten Commandments being given to God's people;
- learn about the Greatest Commandment;
- explore the role of the rules and guidelines in living a safe, healthy, and good life; and
- consider how to put God at the center of their lives.

Bible Story

Moses goes up Mount Sinai to listen to God and bring back guidelines for living in right relationship with God and with community. (Exodus 19:1-8, 16-20; 20:1-21; 24:3-18; 34:27-35)

Bible Verse

Then God spoke all these words: I am the LORD your God who brought you out of Egypt, out of the house of slavery. You must have no other gods before me. (Exodus 20:1-3)

Focus for the Teacher

The Ten Commandments are so much more than a relic from history or an ancient set of dos and don'ts. When you look at each of the "words," the principles that lay behind them, and the way Jesus spoke to them and lived them, you'll find that they are far more relevant to your life than you imagined. Far from being burdens meant to rob us of our joy, they are words of life: guideposts and guardrails aimed at helping us experience the goodness and beauty that God intended.

—Adam Hamilton

You probably remember the Exodus story that traces the life of Moses from his birth and survival of the pharaoh's murderous edicts through his growing up in the palace to his defense of the Hebrew people to his meeting God in a burning bush. All of that, as well as the Hebrews' survival after crossing the sea following Moses out of Egyptian servitude, is the setting for the story of the Ten Commandments.

Words of Life divides the Ten Commandments into two sections. The first four commandments address humanity's relationship with God, setting guidelines for how to be in right relationship with the Divine. The last six commandments address humanity's relationships with one another, setting guidelines for how to live in a safe and healthy community. Jesus summarized the commandments, as well as all the laws of the Torah (the first five books of the Bible), in quoting Deuteronomy 6:5, "Love the LORD your God with all your heart, all your being, and all your strength," and Leviticus 19:18b, "love your neighbor as yourself." It may be helpful throughout these sessions to refer to the Greatest Commandment and invite the children to reflect if the Ten Commandments help them live faithfully with the Greatest Commandment.

The first commandment can be read as a key to all the other commandments. "I am the LORD your God.... You must have no other gods before me" (Exodus 20:2a-3). In this commandment, God is claiming the Israelites as God's own people. In Egypt, where the Israelites had just left, there were many gods and many ways to worship those gods. Here, God is calling the Israelites to recognize the covenant God had made long ago with Abraham and to recognize the one God as the focus of their worship and praise. In this first commandment, God is giving the Israelites a sense of identity and purpose, directing them toward God as their highest allegiance.

Explore Interest Groups

Adult leaders should prepare the space before the children arrive. When children arrive, welcome them by name and invite them into the space. Briefly give them a choice of activities and set clear time boundaries. For children struggling with transitions, it can be helpful to have a timer set and be able to give an estimate of the length of time activities will take.

Greatest Commandment Coloring Page (Younger Children)

- Invite younger children to make themselves comfortable at a table. Give them each a copy of Resource Page 1-1 and help them read the words in the middle. Have the children color in the words.

Prepare

- ✓ **Supplies:** Resource Page 1-1, crayons, markers
- ✓ Make copies of Resource Page 1-1.

Images of God Coloring Page (Older Children)

- Invite older children to make themselves comfortable at a table. Give them each a copy of Resource Page 1-2 and a Bible. Help them look up the Scripture passages. Have them draw the images of God named in the passages in the blank space.

Prepare

- ✓ **Supplies**: Copies of Resource Page 1-2, crayons, markers
- ✓ Make copies of Resource Page 1-2.

Clay Tablets (All Ages)

- Give each child a paper plate and have them label it with his or her name.
- Give each child a chunk of clay (about 5 oz.) and direct them to roll it out and flatten it. Help them use a Popsicle stick to carve the clay into two tablet shapes.
- Give each child a toothpick. Have them write the numbers from 1 to 4 on one of the tablets and 5 to 10 on the other tablet.
- Allow children to decorate the clay with markers.
- Set aside to let air dry.

Prepare

- ✓ **Supplies:** Air-dry clay (such as Crayola Air-Dry Clay), paper plates, markers, Popsicle sticks, toothpicks
- ✓ Cover a table with plastic or a tablecloth. Prepare the clay according to directions on the package. Make an example before the session.

Love the Lord Key (All Ages)

- Give each child a copy of Resource Page 1-3. Invite them to connect the dots on the page.
- **SAY:** This is in the shape of a key because this commandment is the most important thing to remember about being a Christian. These directions are the most important rules for living in the world with love, justice, and peace.

Prepare

- ✓ **Supplies:** copies of Resource Page 1-3, pencils, crayons, markers
- ✓ Make copies of Resource Page 1-3.

Large Group (All Together)

Bring all the children together to experience the Bible story. Ring jingle bells to alert the children to the large group time.

Prepare

✓ **Supplies:** Bible (*Deep Blue Kids* suggested), posterboard, markers

✓ Write the Bible verse on the posterboard.

Bible Story

• Gather the children into a circle.

• **SAY:** I am going to give you directions and I want you to follow me the best you can.

• Give the following directions, first speaking slowly and carefully, then getting faster and faster.

• **SAY:** Stand in a circle. Put your hands on your head. Turn around. Stand on one leg. Stand up straight. Take your hands off your head. Move your head in a circle. Blink your eyes. Give someone a high five. Sit down.

• **ASK:** Was it hard to follow my directions? Why? Why not? What made it challenging?

• Allow the children time to respond.

• **SAY:** For the next few weeks we will be reading about how God gave God's people some directions to follow. Well, actually there were a lot of directions, but there are ten directions that are the most important. These are called the Ten Commandments.

• Invite children to listen as you read aloud Exodus 19:1-8, 16-20; 20:1-21; 24:3-18; 34:27-35.

• **ASK:** Who can remember where Moses went in the story? What did Moses take with him? What did Moses bring back?

• **SAY:** Moses listened to God's rules and then shared them with God's people. Rules might sound boring sometimes, but they can also be helpful for a group of people to know how they relate to one another and how they need to behave. These rules, the Ten Commandments, helped God's people know how to live together as a healthy community.

• Refer to the Bible verse poster.

• Have the children read the Bible verse poster together in a loud voice.

Categorizing the Commandments

- Place the slips of paper with the Ten Commandments printed on them in a central location that can be accessed by the children.

- SAY: The Ten Commandments can be thought about in two sections. Some of the commandments have to do with how humans relate to God. And some of the commandments have to do with how humans relate to one another.

- Ask a child to select one of the commandments and read it to the class. Invite a brief discussion about what category that commandment should be placed in. Have the child tape the commandment in the correct category. Continue until all of the commandments have been placed on the large piece of paper by the children.

- As each child tapes the commandment on the chart, talk about why some commandments can be categorized easily and some are harder. Lead the children to tape the commandments 1 to 4 on the "Relationship with God" side and commandments 5 to 10 on the "Relationship with people" side.

Prepare

✓ **Supplies:** Resource Page 1-4, scissors, large paper, markers, tape

✓ Cut out each commandment from Resource Page 1-4. Divide a large piece of paper into two sections by drawing a vertical line down the middle. Label the two sides "Relationship with God" and "Relationship with people."

The Greatest Commandment

- Gather the children at the prepared tables. Give each child a sheet of plain paper and a white crayon. Invite them to copy "I am the LORD your God. You shall have no other gods before me" from the Bible verse poster onto their paper in white crayon. (An adult or older child may need to help younger children copy the words.)

- Have the children use watercolor paints to paint around and over the white crayon writing. The white crayon will show through the watercolors.

- SAY: This first commandment is important because it shows the relationship God has with God's people. This is something that can never be taken away or covered up. God is our God, and we should not treat anything else in the world or in our lives like it is our God. When Jesus lived (a long time after Moses), Jesus remembered this commandment and was even more specific. He said that we should love God with our whole heart, mind, soul, and strength. This commandment is something called the Greatest Commandment.

- Invite children who completed the Love the Lord Key connect the dots page to share their drawings.

- SAY: Each week when we learn about another commandment, remember that this is the first commandment, the key to understanding all of them.

Prepare

✓ **Supplies:** plain cardstock or watercolor paper, white crayons, watercolor paint, cups of water, paintbrushes

✓ Cover a table with plastic or newspaper to make a clean workspace. Fill cups with water.

Small Groups

Divide the children into small groups. You may organize around age levels or around readers and nonreaders. Keep the groups small, with a maximum of ten children in each group. You may need to have more than one of each group.

You Are Included (Younger Children)

- **SAY:** The first commandment was God's way of telling the Israelites that they were God's people, that they were included and belonged with God. If the Israelites obeyed God's commandments, that showed God that they accepted God as theirs.

- **ASK:** What does it feel like to be included? (for example, when someone invites you to play with them, when you get to help your family, feeling good to be part of something, and so on)

- Direct the children to turn to a friend and create a "secret handshake." Explain that secret handshakes are one of the ways that people are included in groups and feel like they belong.

- **ASK:** What can you do to include people in God's family? How will you worship God as the first commandment says?

Prepare

✓ **Supplies:** Images of God coloring page (Resource Page 1-2), crayons, markers

✓ Complete the Images of God coloring page as an example.

Images of God (Older Children)

- **SAY:** The first commandment has God tell God's people that they should worship only God. This means that nothing else should be as important in their lives as God. In Bible times, different groups of people worshipped different gods. So the first commandment also showed the Israelites who their God was. That's kind of complicated, because God is bigger than anyone can imagine. So the Israelites, the people of God, tried to describe God using different pictures from their imagination.

- Invite children who completed the Images of God coloring page to share their pages. If none have completed this activity, show them your completed page.

- **SAY:** In the Bible, there is a story about Moses meeting God on a mountaintop. God says that God's name is "I am" or "I will be what I will be." That's a confusing name! But this name of God has meaning. This name "I am" expresses how big and mysterious God is.

- **ASK:** What other images of God do we know from the Bible?

- **ASK:** What images would you add to the list? How do you imagine God?

Closing Worship (All Ages)

Bring all the children back together into the large group for closing worship.

Ten Commandments Mobile

- Print Resource Page 1-4 and glue it onto a backing of cardstock.

- Cut out the prologue card and use a hole punch to put a string through it and attach it to the center of the mobile under the X.

- Cut out the first commandment and be ready to attach it during the session.

- Invite children to gather and sit comfortably in a circle.

- **SAY:** Whenever we are trying to live by God's rules, we need to find balance. God loves us all the time, but God knows we are human and we make mistakes, So we need to try our best.

- Show the mobile to the children with the prologue cut out and hung in the middle. Explain that this is the center of all of the commandments, the part where God claims God's people.

- Add the first commandment to one of the branches of the mobile.

- **SAY:** Today we learned that the Ten Commandments are rules that help us live in healthy relationship with God and with other people. The first commandment is about belonging with God and promising to worship God only. Nothing should be more important in our lives than our relationship with God.

- **ASK:** How can you put God first in your life? How do you worship God? How does worshipping God help you live in good relationship with other people?

- **PRAY:** *Holy God, thank you for creating us and calling us your people. We love you and worship you. We will do our best to live as Jesus taught us. Help us show your love to the world. Amen.*

Prepare

- ✓ **Supplies:** two dowels or 2–3' twigs, string, cardstock, scissors, hole punch, glue, Resource Page 1-4

- ✓ Tie the two dowels/twigs together in an X with the string. Use the string to make a hanging loop about 2' long so the twigs hang horizontally.

- ✓ **Tip:** Hold on to the cardstock backed print of Resource Page 1-4. You will need it for all of your sessions.

The Greatest Commandment

You shall love the Lord your God with all your heart, with all your soul, and with all your might. (Deuteronomy 6:5)

Images of God Coloring Page

1 John 4:8

Psalm 18:2

Hebrews 3:4

Love the Lord Key

You shall love
the LORD your God
with all your heart,
with all your soul,
and with all
your might.

Ten Commandments Mobile

I am the LORD your God,
who brought you out of the land of
Egypt, out of the house of slavery;

I. You shall have no other gods before me.

II. You shall not make for yourself an idol.

III. You shall not make wrongful use of the name of the Lord your God.

IV. Remember the Sabbath day, and keep it holy.

V. Honor your father and your mother.

VI. You shall not murder.

VII. You shall not commit adultery.

VIII. You shall not steal.

IX. You shall not bear false witness against your neighbor.

X. You shall not covet.

2. The Idols We Keep

Objectives

The children will:

- hear the story of God's people making an idol,
- explore God's commandment not to make idols,
- consider how God's presence on earth is represented in their lives and in organized worship spaces, and
- discern between loving something and worshipping it as if it were God.

Bible Story

Moses returns from Mount Sinai to find God's people had made an idol. (Exodus 32:1-20)

Bible Verse

Do not make an idol for yourself—no form whatsoever—of anything in the sky above or on the earth below or in the waters under the earth. Do not bow down to them or worship them. (Exodus 20:4-5)

Focus for the Teacher

What are the things that are most important to you? The second commandment, prohibiting the worship of idols, calls us to look at the importance of God in our lives. Sometimes it is easy to avoid thinking about how we are arranging our lives. With family, church, work, school, and community obligations, who has time to make sure God is at the center?

The church sanctuary is a good place to start in your journey of checking to make sure God's love is at the center of your life. Worship spaces can show you a lot about what is important to a community of faith. Is the Word of God honored, shown by a Bible in a prominent place or a central location where the preacher stands? Is contemplation and prayer important, with places to light a candle or prayer cards or tools for reflection? Take a look at your worship space and notice how it is organized. Likewise, you can look at your home, your workspace, or your schedule and see what it gives prominence to. Similarly, explore your children's group space. How does the physical space communicate the importance of God to the children who learn there?

The Bible story today, accompanying the second commandment, is about what the Israelites did while Moses was on the top of Mount Sinai listening to God. Enabled by Aaron,

Moses's brother, the people made a metal image of a calf for the people to worship. In ancient times, people sometimes carried small idols with them or displayed them in their houses. This golden calf was a large representation of those small idols . . . and the people began to worship it. Of course, God was not pleased, and Moses was not pleased, and the people had some learning to do about how properly to worship God and no other being.

It's okay to feel some sympathy for the Israelite people. They were in a tough position: they had been through a lot and they wanted a reminder of God's presence with them. And sometimes we, too, want signs of God's strength and power and love with us. That's why symbols like the cross, the tree of life, or a church steeple are important to us. The problem is if we begin to worship those things themselves, and not the all-powerful, wonderful God they point to.

Today we can be tempted to worship things other than God. Love, money, power, social status, even our country. But all of these things are nothing compared to God's love and mercy in our lives. As you lead the children though the lesson today, share God's grace with them as you all seek to put God at the center of your lives and worship.

Explore Interest Groups

Adult leaders should prepare the space before the children arrive. When children arrive, welcome them by name and invite them into the space. Briefly give them a choice of activities and set clear time boundaries. For children struggling with transitions, it can be helpful to have a timer set and be able to give an estimate of the length of time activities will take.

Forty Days and Forty Nights (Younger Children)

- Have children make forty dots to symbolize the forty days and nights that Moses was up on Mount Sinai with God.

- Direct the children to make the forty dots in any pattern they want (maybe 8 × 5 grid, a pinwheel shape, or the shape of a mountain).

- **SAY:** When we are trying to listen to God, it can take time. In our Bible story today we will learn how Moses took a long time listening to God, trying to understand what God wanted him to do. Moses took forty days! So when you make forty dots on this paper, remember that it takes time to listen and understand what God wants.

Prepare

✓ **Supplies:** plain paper, paint, circular sponge brush (use finger paint if desired)

✓ Make an example.

Making an Ark (All Ages)

- Give each child a craft box. Direct them to decorate the boxes as they each desire.

- **SAY:** When Moses was on the mountain listening to God, God told him how to make a special box. This special box was called an "ark" and it was like a throne for God on earth. God gave Moses exact instructions for making this ark. The box that you are making can be a reminder of how God's people honored God's presence on earth by making a special ark.

Prepare

✓ **Supplies:** small craft boxes, jewel stickers, markers, glue, battery-operated candles, small plastic or paper hearts

✓ Make an example.

Large Group (All Ages)

Bring all the children together to experience the Bible story. Ring jingle bells to alert the children to the large group time.

Prepare

✓ **Supplies:** Bible (*Deep Blue Kids* suggested), posterboard, markers

✓ Write the Bible verse on the posterboard.

Bible Story

- Invite the children to gather into a circle and sit comfortably.
- **ASK:** What are the Ten Commandments? Where did they come from?
- **SAY:** The Ten Commandments were a gift to God's people from God. Moses listened to God and told the people what God said. The commandments are guidelines to help people have a good relationship with God and a good relationship with one another.
- Show the children the Bible verse poster. Invite them to repeat the Bible verse aloud three times.
- **SAY:** This Bible verse says that God doesn't want us to make idols of anything. This means that God doesn't want us to worship something other than God. Nothing should be more important to us than God. God's love is the center of our lives.
- Read Exodus 32:1-14 aloud from a Bible. Invite a child who reads to help if desired.
- **SAY:** Moses told God's people about the rules God gave them for living together in community. But then, they decided to make a statue of a calf to worship, instead of worshipping God.
- **ASK:** Why did the people want to make a statue? Why did Aaron, Moses's brother, give in to what they asked? What was God's response to this violation of the second commandment? How did Moses convince God to change God's mind?
- **SAY:** Maybe we don't feel like we want to worship a golden statue, but we do sometimes want to make other things more important than God in our lives. Sometimes we focus so much on something it can be like an idol. For example, some people talk about the Bible as if they worship it. The Bible is a special book, but the Bible is not God. We should treat it as special, but we don't need to worship it or love it like we love God.
- **ASK:** What in your life do you pay so much attention to that you might want to worship it? (for example, getting toys, being loved, getting good grades, and so forth.)
- **SAY:** God wants us to live in a balanced way, so we are practicing good relationships with God and with other people in our community. If we remember the second commandment, we remember that we should only worship God, not popularity or grades or possessions or money.

In My Worship Space

- Give each child a copy of Resource Page 2-1, writing implements, and a clipboard (if available).

- Visit the sanctuary in your church. Look at all of the things that represent God or facilitate connection with God in the sanctuary.

- Have each child write or draw responses to the prompts in the boxes.

- Encourage families to visit other houses of worship and see what their worship space says about how they worship and what is important in their faith.

Prepare

✓ **Supplies:** Resource Page 2-1, pencils, crayons, clipboards (if available)

✓ Make copies of Resource Page 2-1.

Virtual Tours of Sacred Space

- Explore these sacred spaces:
  o *Stonehenge, UK:* https://www.360cities.net/image/stonehenge
  o *Notre Dame Cathedral:* https://www.360cities.net/image/notre-dame-de-paris
  o *Church of the Holy Sepulchre:* https://www.360cities.net/image/golgotha-church-of-the-holy-sepulchre-jerusalem
  o *Dome of the Rock, Jerusalem:* https://www.360cities.net/image/dome-of-the-rock-jerusalem
  o *Nasir Al Mulk Mosque, Shiraz, Iran:* https://www.360cities.net/image/nasir-al-mulk-mosque-shiraz
  o *Western Wall, Jerusalem:* https://www.360cities.net/image/westetn-wall-jerusalem
  o *Golden Temple:* https://www.360cities.net/image/golden-temple-3

- **ASK:** What similarities do these sacred spaces have? What differences?

- **SAY:** In each religious tradition, people try to find ways to feel close to and worship their God. When we worship, we shape our religious spaces to show different characteristics of God that are important to us. But we always have to be careful not to make the worship space more important than the God we are worshipping.

Prepare

✓ **Supplies:** computer or another internet-connected device

✓ Load the websites for the sacred spaces listed on the left.

Small Groups

Divide the children into small groups. You may organize around age levels or around readers and nonreaders. Keep the groups small, with a maximum of ten children in each group. You may need to have more than one of each group.

Prepare

✓ **Supplies:** *Maybe God Is Like That, Too* by Jennifer Grant

Prepare

✓ **Supplies:** large sheet of paper or whiteboard, markers

God's Love (Younger Children)

- **SAY:** In the Bible, God gave the Ten Commandments as a way of reminding the Israelites how to live. God also gave Moses directions for how to make an ark, a special box that reminded God's people that God was with them on earth. As Christians, we don't believe that anything humanmade actually is God. Instead, we have reminders in our churches and when we gather that God is present with us. We can also look around at the world and find people and actions that remind us of God's love.

- **Read:** *Maybe God Is Like That, Too.*

- **ASK:** Have you ever experienced God like the child in the book does? Who reminds you of God? Who shows you God's love?

- **SAY:** We don't need to worship anything other than God. But we can look for signs of God in the world and in people around us.

The Most Important Things in Your Life (Older Children)

- Invite children to sit in a circle. Have each of them turn to a friend nearby. Direct them to tell their partners what the three most important things in their lives are. Give them five minutes to share with each other.

- Invite children to share with the whole group. Write what they share on the large sheet of paper or whiteboard.

- After everyone who wants to share has shared, observe aloud what kinds of things are named as important (for example, "I see that family is important to a lot of us" or "I see that a lot of us love our stuffed animals " and so on)

- **ASK:** What is the difference between loving something and worshipping something? Are the things we love all things we can see? Are they things that we feel?

- **SAY:** Even though we can't see it, we know that love is real. We know kindness is real. And we know God is real. We can see clues of how all of these things exist in our everyday lives.

- **ASK:** Is seeing believing? Or the other way around?

Closing Worship (All Ages)

Bring all the children back together into the large group for closing worship.

Ten Commandments Mobile

✓ **SAY:** The Ten Commandments are rules that help us live in healthy relationships with God and with other people. The first four commandments help us have a good relationship with God. Last session we learned that the first commandment told us to worship only God. This session we learned that the second commandment tells us that we should keep God at the center of our lives and not get distracted by making something else too important.

• Add the second commandment to the Ten Commandments Mobile.

• **ASK:** How does the second commandment help us have a good relationship with God? Why is it important that God is at the center of our lives? If something else in our lives becomes too important, what happens to our relationship with God?

• **SAY:** God loves us all the time. That's why the Ten Commandments are important. Rules help us live healthy and safe lives.

• **ASK:** How does the second commandment to not make idols help us live healthy and safe lives?

• **PRAY:** *Holy God, thank you for giving us guidelines so that we can have a relationship with you. Give us the wisdom to know when we are making something else too important in our lives and to turn back to you. Help us put you at the center of our lives and see your work in the world every day. Amen.*

Prepare

✓ **Supplies:** Ten Commandments Mobile, Resource Page 1-4 from chapter 1, hole punch, string

✓ Cut out the second commandment and put a string through it with a hole punch.

In My Worship Space

I hear...

I taste...

I smell...

I feel...

I see...

3. Respecting God's Name

Objectives

The children will:

- hear Jesus's teaching about salt and light;
- reflect on the meaning of names, including God's name;
- consider what it means to be an example for others of someone who follows God; and
- plan how they can shine God's light in the world through their words and action.s

Bible Story

Jesus calls his followers salt and light during the Sermon on the Mount. (Matthew 5:13-16)

Bible Verse

Do not use the LORD your God's name as if it were of no significance; the LORD won't forgive anyone who uses his name that way.

(Exodus 20:7)

Focus for the Teacher

When you were a kid, did you ever experiment with cursing? Were you ever told not to "take the Lord's name in vain"? Well, this is where that admonition comes from. The third commandment says, according to the Common English Bible, "Do not use the LORD your God's name as if it were of no significance." This wording helps us get closer to the historical context of the commandment, which is likely more about misrepresenting God, or using God's name as a false oath, and less about cursing as we think of it today.

God's name is a big deal in the Bible. We first encounter God's name as Moses reaches the burning bush in Exodus 3:14. God says "I Am Who I Am," which is sometimes translated as "I WILL BE WHO I WILL BE." This might seem cryptic or confusing, but the closest way we can understand the meaning of these phrases today is that God transcends time (and grammar!). Adam Hamilton suggests that he understands God's name as "'I Am BEING itself.' Or 'Everything that exists derives its existence from me.' Or perhaps best, 'I am the Source and Sustainer of *everything*.'" You probably have heard that God's name is "Yahweh," but we don't find that word in the Bible all the time. Instead, the word LORD is substituted. Why is that? It's actually because of the third commandment! Scribes were so worried about

using the name of God improperly that they decided it's best just to leave the holy name out. Whenever you read the word LORD in all caps or small caps in the Bible, know that it is a substitute for God's name, which is too holy to repeat. Many Jewish people today don't say or write "God" out of respect for the name. Instead, they may write "G-d." How we treat names is important.

The third commandment reminds us that we are representatives of God on earth. If we speak poorly about God, or use God's name lightly, we are not respecting God, and thus, we show others that it's okay to disrespect God. Instead, think about how you want people to respect God. How can you be an example of honoring God (and God's name) by your words and actions?

It's not only God's name that is important. Each child you lead has a name and a story and a history. During this session's activities, reflect on the importance of names and what they show us about relationships and identity. Our identity as Christians is important, as is represented in the song "They'll Know We Are Christians by Our Love." Today, focus on knowing the names and individual stories of the children with whom you are ministering. They will know you, and know God, through your love.

Explore Interest Groups

Adult leaders should prepare the space before the children arrive. When children arrive, welcome them by name and invite them into the space. Briefly give them a choice of activities and set clear time boundaries. For children struggling with transitions, it can be helpful to have a timer set and be able to give an estimate of the length of time activities will take.

Representing God Wheel (Older Children)

- Give each child two paper plates. Have them divide both paper plates into eight sections by drawing straight lines across the paper plates. One plate should have the lines on the front of the plate (that is curved like you would serve food on it). The other plate should have the lines on the back of the plate (so the curve of the plate is facing down).
- Have the children cut one of the wedges out of the plate with the lines on the back.
- On the plate with the lines on the front, have the children cut out and glue the actions on Resource Page 3-1. If some of the actions don't apply to the child (like feeding a pet), invite them to draw another kind of action.
- Attach the plates together so that they nest inside each other, with the plate missing a wedge on the top. Use a brass brad to attach the plates together through the center of the plates.
- Invite the children to write "How I show God's love to the world" on the top plate. The children should be able to turn the top plate so that the images on the bottom plate show through in the cut-out wedge space.
- **SAY:** God gave us the Ten Commandments as guidelines that show us how to live well. Wherever we are in our lives, we can show God's love to the world by our actions. If you need a reminder of how to show God's love, you can use this wheel to decide what you can do. And, you can add even more actions that show God's love to the world!

Beaded Cross Necklace (All Ages)

- **SAY:** Today we are talking about the third commandment. This commandment helps us be aware of how we are representing God. Wherever we are, whether at home or church or out in the world, we want to make sure that we are sharing God's love and being a good example to others of God's love. Sometimes necklaces or bracelets can help us remember to be good representatives.
- Using the instructions on the free tutorial in the margin, show the children how to make either a cross pendant, a necklace, or both.

Prepare
- ✓ **Supplies:** paper plates, brass brads, scissors, pencils, crayons, markers, Resource Page 3-1
- ✓ Make an example. Make copies of Resource Page 3-1.

Prepare
- ✓ **Supplies:** pony beads, ribbon or string, glue dots, and scissors
- ✓ Look at this tutorial (https://www.catholicicing.com/how-to-bead-a-cross-fun-christian-craft/). You may wish to have this video available for kids to watch as you make this together.
- ✓ **Optional:** Pre-glue the center 3 beads as described in the tutorial for younger children; older children should be able to glue the beads themselves.

Large Group (All Ages)

Bring all the children together to experience the Bible story. Ring jingle bells to alert the children to the large group time. Use the transition activity to move the children from the interest groups to the large group area.

Prepare

✓ **Supplies:** Bible (*Deep Blue Kids*), posterboard, markers

✓ Write the Bible verse on the posterboard.

Bible Story

- Gather the children in a circle and have them be seated comfortably.
- Read Matthew 5:13-16 aloud.
- **ASK:** What did Jesus mean when he said "you are the light of the world"? What does light do?
- Have the children read the Bible verse poster aloud three times. The first time, direct them to read it softly in a whisper voice. Then get louder and louder.
- **SAY:** The third commandment reminds us that God's name is special and we need to honor God by treating it as special. This means that what we say about God needs to be respectful and kind. And, how we act needs to show God's love to others. This is what Jesus meant by saying that his followers are "lights" and "cities on a hill." We are representing God and can affect what people know and think about God.

Prepare

✓ **Supplies:** small clear jar (like a baby food jar), glitter glue, paintbrush, battery-operated tea light candle

✓ Make an example. If desired, let families know ahead of time to send a small jar with their child to this session. Cover a workspace with a tablecloth or some plastic to protect the table.

Night Light

- Give each child a jar, a paintbrush, glitter glue, and a small battery-operated tea light candle.
- Have each child use the paintbrush to paint glitter glue on the inside of the clear jar.
- As it dries, **SAY:** In our Bible story today, Jesus told his followers to be a light on a hill for all to see. This means that people who follow Jesus are supposed to be good examples to the world, sharing God's love with everyone. By saying this, Jesus shows us how to follow the third commandment. If we are trying to follow God, we must represent God well and share God's love with the world through our words and our actions.
- **ASK:** What can you do to share God's love? How can you be a light? Who is a light for you?
- Place the jar upside-down over the battery-operated tea light candle.

Simon Says

- **SAY:** We are going to play Simon Says. Except this will be (YOUR NAME) Says. Whenever I say "(YOUR NAME) says…" then you have to do the action. If I don't say "(YOUR NAME) says…" you don't have to do the action. Just try your best, you don't have to be perfect at this game!

- Lead the children in playing (YOUR NAME) Says by giving them directions like the following: put your hand on your head, jump up and down, touch your nose, and so on. After five minutes of playing this game, invite the children to be seated again.

- **SAY:** You all did really well! It is not easy to follow what someone is telling you. And it is even harder to try to figure out how to behave when you are trying to listen for the right direction to follow. This kind of game reminds me that it can be hard to follow the Ten Commandments. It can be hard to follow Jesus, too! We might know in our head that we need to follow God's directions, but it's not always easy. Luckily, God knows that we are humans and we make mistakes—and God loves us all the time! The important thing is that we are doing our best to try and behave the way God wants us to. When people see us sharing love and kindness and justice, we are representing God well and they will know that.

Small Groups

Divide the children into small groups. You may organize around age levels or around readers and nonreaders. Keep the groups small, with a maximum of ten children in each group. You may need to have more than one of each group.

Prepare

✓ **Supplies:** yellow construction paper, scissors, glue or tape, markers

✓ Make an example. Cut out circles about 6" in diameter from the yellow construction paper. Use the leftovers to cut out rectangles 2" × 5".

Prepare

✓ **Supplies:** construction paper, scissors, glue, markers

✓ Make an example, either using your name or "Jesus."

Shining God's Light in the World (Younger Children)

- Give each child a circle and six rectangles. Invite each of them to draw or write in the rectangles something that they want to do to shine God's light in the world (for example, "share," "help," "love," "be kind,"). Then have them glue the six rectangles along the edge of the circle, making a yellow paper sun to signify light.

- **SAY:** Whenever we see this sunshine, we remember that Jesus told us to shine God's light and share God's love in the world. It might be hard sometimes, but this is part of how we live by the third commandment. We want to share God's love and represent God well.

Respecting God's Name (Older Children)

- **SAY:** The third commandment tells us that God's name is important. It is so important that we need to respect it.

- **ASK:** How do you think we should respect God's name? What should we not say? What should we do instead?

- **SAY:** God's name is so special to some people, like people who practice the Jewish religion, that they don't ever write out the whole name of God. Instead, they might use the word LORD or even just put a dash mark when they write. That is how they show their respect for the special name. For Christians, we can say the word *God* as long as we are respectful when we say it. And that's not the only name that is important to respect! Each of us was named and each of us is special. We should respect one another's names, too.

- Give each child two differently colored pieces of construction paper. Instruct them to write their names in big letters on one color, then cut out the letters. Have each chold glue the letters to the other sheet of construction paper so that his or her name name is spelled vertically on the paper. Then, help each child make an acrostic poem where each letter of the child's name begins a word that describes the child.

- Invite the children to share their creations with one another.

Closing Worship (All Ages)

Bring all the children back together into the large group for closing worship.

Ten Commandments Mobile

- Invite the children to share their artistic creations if desired.

- **SAY:** God gave us the Ten Commandments to show us how to live in a healthy and safe relationship with God and with other people. Today we learned about the third commandment, which tells us that what we say about God matters. We should not use God's name to swear or to make promises that are too big. We need to try to show kindness to all people we meet because that is a good way to show how God loves us.

- Add the third commandment to the mobile by attaching it with string.

- **SAY:** Remember that the Ten Commandments are all about balance. They are guidelines for living so that we can have good relationships with God and with our community.

- **ASK:** How do you want to represent God to the world? How will you use kind words and actions to show God's light?

- **SAY:** You might have noticed so far that many of the commandments tell us about what *not* to do. But for every *not* there is a flip side. Telling us *not* to speak God's name carelessly means that we should be careful how we represent God. As we continue to learn about the Ten Commandments, see if you can figure out what the two sides of the commandment are, the *do not* side as well as the *do* side.

- **PRAY:** *Holy God, thank you for showing us the two sides of each commandment. We praise you and respect you, and we ask that you help us represent your love to the world. When we get distracted by unhelpful things, remind us that we should have you at the center of our lives and that we should live so that others can see how you love all of Creation. Amen.*

Prepare

✓ **Supplies:** device to play music, third commandment cut out from Resource Page 1-4 from chapter 1, string, hole punch, Ten Commandments Mobile

✓ Cue the song "They'll Know We Are Christians by Our Love" on your music-playing device. If desired, write the lyrics on a poster and have instruments ready for the kids to use. Cut out the third commandment from Resource Page 1-4 from chapter 1. Use a hole punch to put string through it.

Representing God Wheel

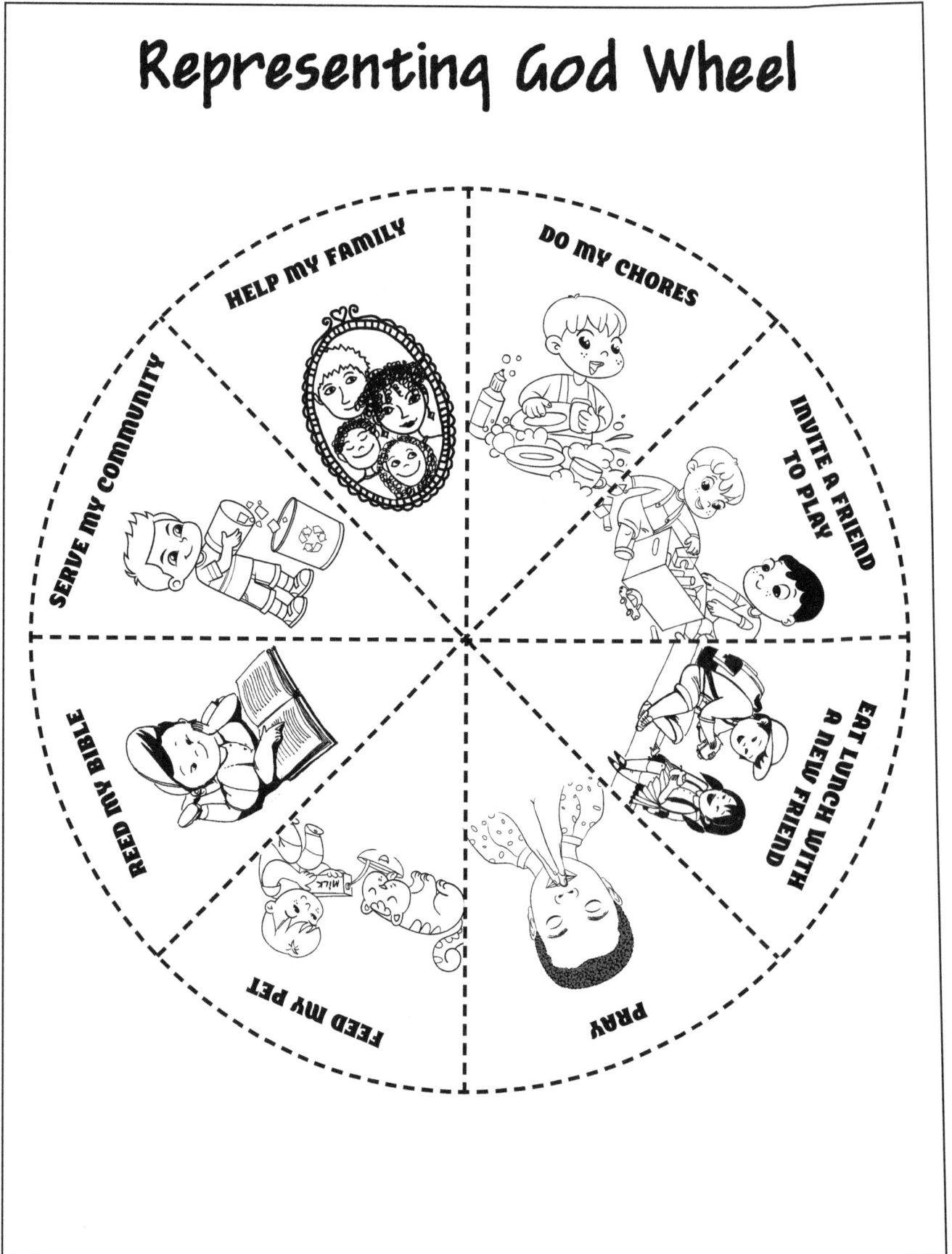

4. Rediscovering the Power of Sabbath

Objectives

The children will:

- hear the story of jubilee and sabbath rest for the land,
- dream of what a time of jubilee would be like today,
- learn about the importance of Sabbath rest, and
- plan how they can encourage others around them to take breaks to rest and worship God.

Bible Story

The story of periodic rest for the land and all people. (Leviticus 25:1-10a; 26:2-13)

Bible Verse

Remember the Sabbath day and treat it as holy. Six days you may work and do all your tasks, but the seventh day is a Sabbath to the LORD your God. (Exodus 20:8-10)

Focus for the Teacher

During the last session, you considered what it means to be a representative of God. Part of representing God is living how God wants us to live, meaning that we must follow God's example and directions given to us in the Ten Commandments. Well, how do you feel knowing that "remember to rest" is one of them?

American work culture is honestly not the healthiest, with many people working really hard with much less time off than in other countries. Adults today are overworked . . . and many children aren't far behind. Between school, clubs, sports, after-school programs, church, family commitments, and hanging out with friends, it can be hard for children today to slow down. The fourth commandment is perhaps the most obviously relevant commandment that you will study in these sessions, and it can have a great impact on your group's well-being.

When some speak about the fourth commandment to "remember the Sabbath day, and keep it holy," some will also say, "God rested and so should you." And it's true! During the creation of all things in Genesis 1, God rested on the seventh day. And in the Gospels that tell us about Jesus's life, Jesus also rested. Humans have to follow this example! Otherwise we will burn out and not have the energy or willpower to do much of anything, not even worship our God.

The Bible story today is about rest, but it's a pretty dramatic form of rest. In Leviticus a time of rest was allotted every seven years (following the pattern of resting on the seventh day) for all people and the whole land to rest and be restored. Then, every fiftieth year would be a jubilee, where there would be forgiveness of debts, rest from work, and free sharing of food. Rest is pretty radical for people who are close to burnout, and the year of sabbath and the jubilee only highlight the extravagant and creative nature of rest for God's people.

As you lead this session, reflect on what example you are setting for the children with whom you are ministering. Are you running yourself ragged? Are you doing this work with joy? Be sure to check in with your pastor and other trusted people to share your feelings and your experiences as a church leader. Children will follow your example, including noticing when you are taking care of yourself! There is no rush for this session. All you have to do is present the information and make a safe space for children to explore and learn. God does the rest. Thanks be to God.

Explore Interest Groups

Adult leaders should prepare the space before the children arrive. When children arrive, welcome them by name and invite them into the space. Briefly give them a choice of activities and set clear time boundaries. For children struggling with transitions, it can be helpful to have a timer set and be able to give an estimate of the length of time activities will take.

Jubilee Collage (Younger Children)

- Invite children to find images of health and joy in the magazines. Have them cut or tear the pictures out.

- **ASK:** What kind of pictures are you looking for that remind you of health? What pictures look joyful to you?

- Give each child a plain sheet of paper and a few clothespins. Instruct them to use the magazines and the clothespins (as people) to create a scene of a healthy world.

- **SAY:** When people get to rest and feel joyful, the whole world feels healthier. Justice and peace are things that come when people have what they need and can rest.

- **ASK:** What does a scene of "justice" look like to you?

- **SAY:** In our Bible story today, we will learn that God wants the whole world to take breaks and rest sometimes. It's good for our health and it's good for the planet. And, even God rested when God was creating the world!

Prepare

- ✓ **Supplies:** plain paper, old-fashioned clothespins, markers, crayons, magazines, glue, scissors

- ✓ Cover a table with a tablecloth or plastic to prepare a workspace. Check the magazines for any inappropriate content.

Restful Sachet (Older Children)

- Give each child two pieces of fabric. Have the child put the wrong sides (the un-patterned sides) together and use the glue to glue the fabric together almost all the way closed (three out of four sides if you are using a square).

- Fill the sachet with the dried herbs and/or potpourri.

- Use fabric glue to close the rest of the sachet.

- **SAY:** God told God's people that there are special days when all of creation should rest. People should take breaks from work, forgive one another, and spend time with people they love. Today, many people work very, very hard and don't have enough breaks. Sometimes we need reminders to take a break and relax. These calming herbs in this sachet can remind us that we need to rest.

Prepare

- ✓ **Supplies:** tightly woven cotton fabric (quilting quarters are good for this), sewing tape or glue, dried herbs or potpourri

- ✓ **Tip:** Be mindful of any allergies in your group.

- ✓ Make an example. If time is an issue, you may wish to pre-cut the fabric into shapes (for example, 6" squares). Cover a workspace with a tablecloth. Have a broom or vacuum available to clean up afterward.

Prepare

✓ **Supplies:** Avery labels or other type of sticker, permanent markers

✓ **Tip:** Find stickers that can be easily removed, such as vinyl stickers. Or, if you do not wish to use stickers, use pieces of cardstock with painters tape.

Good Stickers (All Ages)

- **SAY:** When God created the world, God said that everything God made was very good. Everything from the mountains to rivers to humans to snakes to butterflies to vegetables was good. All of creation was good. In the fourth commandment that we will talk about today, God tells us that rest is important. Everything that God made was good and all of it, even the land, deserves a rest sometimes.

- Give each child several stickers (or cardstock squares) and direct them to write "Very good" on each one with a permanent marker. If using cardstock squares, attach painters tape to the back of each one.

- After the stickers are made, invite the children to look around your classroom (or your whole church) and put stickers on God's creations. You may even want to have children stationed at the church doors to hand out these stickers to people as they leave for the day!

Prepare

✓ **Supplies:** jars (or plastic sandwich bags), wide craft sticks, markers

Jar of Rest (All Ages)

- **SAY:** In the fourth commandment, God told God's people that they should rest. Today, a lot of people work very hard and don't have a lot of breaks. When we take breaks, we have a chance to keep our bodies, minds, and hearts healthy and ready to worship God in our lives. Sometimes we need reminders of how we can rest.

- **ASK:** When do you rest? What activities do you do to rest? Or, what activities do you *not* do while you are resting?

- Give each child a jar and ten craft sticks. Have children write on each craft stick one way they can rest. If needed, suggest the following: read the Bible, pray, take a nap, take a walk, read a book, talk with a loved one, make art. Encourage them to create their own based on how they like to rest! Invite them to take their jars and craft sticks home with them and use them as reminders to rest in specific ways throughout the week.

Large Groups (All Ages)

Bring all the children together to experience the Bible story. Ring jingle bells to alert the children to the large group time.

Bible Story

- Invite children to sit comfortably in a circle.

- **SAY:** Whew! I have been working hard. And you've been working hard, too, on the projects from the beginning of our session.

- Invite any children who want to show their craft to do so.

- **SAY:** It is important to rest. Even God rested, when God was creating the world. So it is not surprising that when God gave the Ten Commandments to God's people, God included that the people should rest, too! And, God even went further than that in another book in the Bible, the Book of Leviticus. Leviticus gives more details about the guidelines that God's people should live by.

- Invite an older reader to read Leviticus 25:1-10a; 26:2-13 aloud.

- **ASK:** When the year of Jubilee happens, who is supposed to rest? Why would God want the land to rest?

- **SAY:** Whenever you hear the word *Sabbath*, you should think of resting. Rest is important because it helps our bodies, minds, and hearts prepare to share God's love with the world. Helping the world be a better place is only possible when we take care of our bodies and set aside time to be with God.

Prepare

✓ **Supplies:** Bible, large posterboard, markers

Hit Pause Tags

- Give each child seven gift tags and seven lengths of ribbon.

- Direct each child to write the word *Pause* on each tag, decorate it, and attach a ribbon to it.

- Encourage the children to take these tags home and tie or tape them somewhere they will see them often. Every time they see one of these tags, encourage them to pause and think about God's plan for God's people to rest.

- **ASK:** Where will you put these tags in your home? What will you do when you see these tags?

Prepare

✓ **Supplies:** blank cardstock gift tags, ribbon, markers

✓ Make an example.

Prepare

✓ **Supplies:** chairs or floor pillows, device for playing music

✓ Arrange chairs or floor pillows in a circle. Make sure there are as many seats as there are children minus one. Cue up a church-appropriate song to play.

Musical Chairs

- Have the children all stand up as they are able. Explain that you will play music and they will walk in a circle around the seats. When you say "Sabbath," they have to find a place to sit and breathe deeply five times. Be sure to keep playing the music. The children have to listen for the word signal instead of the music stopping.

- Ask the child who did not find a place to sit to stand quietly to the side for the remainder of the activity.

- Remove another chair or floor pillow from the circle. Continue the activity for a few more rounds or until only one child is left sitting. At the end of each round, eliminate the child left standing and remove another chair or floor pillow.

- **ASK:** What was it like to listen for the word *Sabbath*? Was it more or less challenging than it would have been to listen for just the music to stop?

- **SAY:** Sometimes the world is really busy, and the activity won't stop. But the fourth commandment tells us that even when the world is really busy, God wants us to rest. God wants us to take time to restore ourselves and worship God.

Small Groups

Divide the children into small groups. You may organize around age levels or around readers and nonreaders. Keep the groups small, with a maximum of ten children in each group. You may need to have more than one of each group.

Time for Sabbath (All Ages)

- Give each child a few sheets of cardstock. Make sure they have access to the assorted art supplies.

- **ASK:** Who is someone in your life who takes care of people? Who do you know who works hard helping others? What do those people who are caretakers need to be rested and feel joy?

- **SAY:** Sometimes people need a reminder to rest, especially people who are used to working really hard and taking care of other people. As we make these cards today, think of persons you need to remind to take a rest. This card will be a reminder to them that they need to take care of themselves so they can help others and do God's work from a place of joy.

- Have the children fold each sheet of cardstock in half, forming a card, write "Time for Sabbath" on the cover of the card, then write a message to a loved one inside and decorate it.

- Here are some suggestions for what to write: "God rested, and you should, too!" "Rest is important. Take a nap!" "Do something that brings you joy." "Serve God from a place of rest and peace."

- If desired, suggest that the children make cards for the pastors and other ministry and lay leaders in your congregation.

Prepare

✓ **Supplies:** cardstock, markers, crayons, glue, assorted art supplies

Closing Worship (All Ages)

Bring all the children back together into the large group for closing worship.

Prepare

✓ **Supplies:** fourth commandment cut out from Resource Page 1-4 from chapter 1, string, hole punch, Ten Commandments Mobile

✓ Cut out the fourth commandment from Resource Page 1-4 from chapter 1. Use a hole punch to make a hole and put string through it.

Ten Commandments Mobile

• Invite the children to share their artistic creations if desired.

• **SAY:** God gave us the Ten Commandments to show us how to live in a healthy and safe relationship with God and with others people. Today we learned that God wants all of creation to rest. Rest is important because it helps people feel restored. When we set aside time to rest, we have more energy for following God's way of love and justice in the world.

• Add the fourth commandment to the mobile by attaching it with string.

• **SAY:** Remember that the Ten Commandments are all about balance. They are guidelines for living so that we can have good relationships with God and with our community.

• **ASK:** How does resting help our relationship with God? How does resting help our relationship with others? How does resting help us care for ourselves?

• **PRAY:** *Holy God, thank you for reminding us to rest. Sometimes we think we are too busy to pay attention to you or to others in need. Help us take time to rest and restore our bodies, minds, and spirits. Help us encourage hardworking grown-ups in our lives to rest, also. Show us the ways to remain connected with you in the midst of our busy lives. Amen.*

5. A Question of Honor

Objectives

The children will:

- hear the commandment to honor one's parents,
- reflect on how elders have helped raise them and how they can honor them in return, and
- recognize the importance of honoring elders and how that is related to worshipping God.

Bible Story

Jesus talks about how honoring elders also honors God. (Matthew 15:1-9)

Bible Verse

Honor your father and your mother so that your life will be long on the fertile land that the LORD your God is giving you.

(Exodus 20:12)

Focus for the Teacher

The fifth commandment begins the second section of commandments that gives guidelines for living well with other people. It might seem simple, but the fifth commandment has wide implications for the organization of a community. Many of us know "honor thy father and mother," and we think, "Okay, we're listening, that's it!" But Adam Hamilton helps us understand that "honoring" isn't just listening and obeying. Honoring is more about committing to helping and protecting our elders as they age, since they first raised us.

In the ancient world, families would live together so that as people aged, the younger family members could care for them. In the United States today, it is becoming less and less common for multiple generations to live together. This practice varies based on socioeconomic status and cultural differences, but in general, many older people live in senior communities, assisted living facilities, or nursing homes. Additionally, many elders are living only on Social Security and Medicare, having to make tough choices about seeking medical treatment, paying for prescriptions, or buying food. Studying the fifth commandment urges us to ask why this is and whether we are honoring our elders with a society that is set up this way.

As you lead your groups in considering the fifth commandment to honor parents, it is incredibly important to be sensitive to the family situations of children in your group. A heartbreaking truth is that some children do not have safe and healthy home lives. They may be victims of emotional, physical, or sexual abuse at the hands of their parents or other adult relatives. They may be living apart from their parents due to addiction, incarceration, or even immigration status. They may be in foster care. Do your best to be sensitive throughout this session and recognize that children may react differently based on their experiences of their elders.

In this session, you are encouraged to explore what it means to "honor." How does "honoring" expand on loving? How can you and the children in your care offer blessings to parents, families, elders, and seniors in your community? There are many things younger people can learn from older people, and treating them as elders who have their own skills and gifts to share can shift children's perspectives on what it means to be in relationship with seniors.

While leading, approach these topics with care and thoughtfulness. Invite children to share their experiences and allow them to dream of what they will be like when they are the elders. Offer yourself as a guide, no matter how old you are, and listen for the wisdom from the mouths of babes as you grow together in making your community a place of honor.

Explore Interest Groups

Adult leaders should prepare the space before the children arrive. When children arrive, welcome them by name and invite them into the space. Briefly give them a choice of activities and set clear time boundaries. For children struggling with transitions, it can be helpful to have a timer set and be able to give an estimate of the length of time activities will take.

Family Portrait (Younger Children)

- **TIP:** Be aware if there are any adopted or foster children in your group, and shape the conversation and activity in a way that makes clear they are included.
- Give each child a sheet of cardstock.
- **ASK:** What is a family? What does "being family" mean to you? Who is in your family?
- Direct the children to use finger paint and markers to create a portrait of their families. Continue to engage with them, asking them who they are drawing and why, and allowing them to think outside their biological family if they choose.

Prepare
- ✓ **Supplies:** plain cardstock, finger paint, markers, plates or trays for paint
- ✓ Make an example. Create a clean workspace by covering a table with plastic or a tablecloth. Prepare plates or trays with the finger paint.

When I'm Older (Older Children)

- **ASK:** Do you ever think about yourself when you are older? What kinds of feelings do you have when you imagine growing up? Are you excited? Are you nervous? scared? anxious?
- **SAY:** It can be important to imagine a vision of what we will be like when we grow up. And we can imagine how we want to get there. Yes, you can just let time pass and you can grow but you also can learn new things. Trying something new is one way to grow!
- **ASK:** What kinds of things do you want to learn that will help you grow?
- Direct the children to illustrate their future selves on the gingerbread person on Resource Page 5-1. Encourage them to fill out the prompts at the top and bottom of the page.
- **SAY:** When we imagine how we want to be when we are older, we have more compassion for people who are older now. This will be important to remember as we think about our Bible story today.

Prepare
- ✓ **Supplies:** Resource Page 5-1, pencils, markers
- ✓ Make copies of Resource Page 5-1.

Honored Tickets (All Ages)

- Give each child a copy of Resource Page 5-2.
- **ASK:** What does *honor* mean? What do you do to "honor" someone?
- **SAY:** Honor is when we treat someone with kindness and respect. Sometimes when someone does something really big they get a special honor, like an award or a medal. But people are doing big deal things every day, so we are going to honor some of those people.
- Invite the children to think of adults in their life that they want to honor. Help the children think of creative ways to honor an adult in their life.
- Have the children fill out the tickets, color them as they like, and cut them apart. Suggest that they present the tickets to those adults.

Prepare
- ✓ **Supplies:** Resource Page 5-2, scissors, markers, crayons, pencils
- ✓ Make copies of Resource Page 5-2.

Large Group (All Ages)

Bring all the children together to experience the Bible story. Ring jingle bells to alert the children to the large group time. Use the transition activity to move the children from the interest groups to the large group area.

Prepare

✓ **Supplies:** posterboard, markers, Bible (*Deep Blue Kids*)

✓ Write the Bible verse on the posterboard.

Bible Verse

- Invite the children to sit in a circle.

- **SAY:** Over the past few sessions we have been learning about the Ten Commandments and how they help us live in right relationship with God and healthy and safe relationships with people. The first four commandments show us how to worship God. The last six commandments help us understand how to live in peace with other people.

- Have the children read the Bible verse from the poster aloud together. Direct them to clap when reading the words *father* and *mother* and *God*.

- **ASK:** We clapped on the words *father*, *mother*, and *God*. What do these roles have in common? What other roles could we add to the list? (for example, "parent," "grandparent," "elders," and so on) How does honoring our elders or our caretakers help us have good relationships with people?

- **SAY:** In our Bible story today, Jesus teaches people that honoring elders is an important part of honoring God. Honoring elders is also part of taking care of a community.

Bible Story

- Invite the children to listen as you read Matthew 15:1-9.

- **ASK:** What does it mean to "honor" someone? How is "honoring" humans different from "worshipping" God? How do we know who we should honor?

- **SAY:** In this Bible story, Jesus tells those listening that honoring elders is one way we honor God, because God commands us to honor elders. So living according to the guidelines of the Ten Commandments is a way we honor God.

Interviewing Our Elders

- Invite a senior Sunday school class to join your class. Or, ask your pastor to help you pair up children and seniors to interview each other.
- Give each child and each senior a copy of Resource Page 5-3. Have them interview each other.

Prepare

✓ **Supplies:** Resource Page 5-3

✓ Make copies of Resource Page 5-3.

Care Packages

- Give each child a sheet of cardstock and encourage each of them to decorate it to give to senior adults.
- Have the children make care packages with the cards, snacks, and other treats.
- If there is time, deliver the care packages to senior Sunday school classes or other groups.
- **ASK:** How do you think the people who receive these gifts will feel? How do you hope they will feel?

Prepare

✓ **Supplies:** gift bags, small snacks and water bottles, cardstock, assorted art supplies

✓ Consult your senior ministries or senior church groups to suggest collaboration with your children's class. You may wish to invite senior Sunday school groups to visit your class so they can work together.

Small Groups

Divide the children into small groups. You may organize around age levels or around readers and nonreaders. Keep the groups small, with a maximum of ten children in each group. You may need to have more than one of each group.

Prepare

✓ **Supplies:** Resource Page 5-4, scissors, crayons, markers

✓ Make copies of Resource Page 5-4.

Matching Game (Younger Children)

- Invite each child to sit down with some space clear in front of each of them on the floor (or at a table).

- Give each child a copy of Resource Page 5-4 and safety scissors. Have them cut the squares on the dotted line.

- After they cut the squares apart, assign the children to groups of two or three. Have one child lay the squares mixed up and facedown on the floor or table in front of their group.

- **ASK:** What are some actions we can do to honor our elders? What do you already do for them? What do you think they will appreciate?

- Invite the children to find all the matches among the cards, taking turns to look at two cards at a time. As each match is found, ask the children to say the match out loud and name someone they could honor in that way (for example, "I could help my grandma in the garden.")

- **ASK:** How does it feel to plan how you will honor your elders?

Prepare

✓ **Supplies:** paper, assorted art materials

✓ If possible, set up a visit with the children's class and a senior living community near the church, or with a senior adult Sunday school class. Match up one or two children with a Senior Buddy. If this is not possible by the time you do this activity, invite the children to do the following:

Senior Buddies (Older Children)

- Give each child a sheet of paper and allow each of them to choose from the art supplies.

- Encourage the children to introduce themselves to their Senior Buddy by writing a letter or creating a picture. If needed, prompt them with the following questions:
  - o Your first name and birthday
  - o Who is in your family?
  - o What do you like to do for a hobby?
  - o What is your favorite time of year?
  - o What do you like to do with your friends?
  - o What is one skill you have? What do you want to learn how to do?
  - o How would you describe yourself in five words?

- **ASK:** What do you think it will be like to have a Senior Buddy? What do you want to learn from them? What do you think you can teach them? How does having a Senior Buddy help honor them?

Closing Worship (All Ages)

Bring all the children back together into the large group for closing worship.

Ten Commandments Mobile

- Invite the children to share their artistic creations if desired.

- **SAY:** God gave us the Ten Commandments to show us how to live in a healthy and safe relationship with God and with people. Today we learned that God wants us to care for the elders in our community, to honor them. We can honor them by listening to them, helping them, and supporting them.

- Add the fifth commandment to the mobile by attaching it with string.

- **SAY:** Remember that the Ten Commandments are all about balance. They are guidelines for living so that we can have good relationships with God and with our community.

- **ASK:** How does honoring our elders create a healthy community? How do you hope to be honored when you are an elder?

- **PRAY:** *Holy God, you show us how to live in community and love one another. Help us listen, share, help, and honor our elders because they help and teach us. Show us how to worship you by honoring others. Amen.*

Prepare

✓ **Supplies:** fifth commandment cutout from Resource Page 1-4 from chapter 1, string, hole punch, Ten Commandments Mobile

✓ Cut out the fifth commandment from Resource Page 1-4 from chapter 1. Use a hole punch to make a hole and put string through it.

When I'm Older

When I'm older, I will know…

When I'm older, I will be…

Honored Tickets

TICKET

TO:

Because:
❑ I love you
❑ I care about you
❑ You are important
❑ You are awesome
❑ You deserve a treat
❑ I want to help you
❑ Other _____

This ticket entitles you to:

FROM:

TICKET

TICKET

TO:

Because:
❑ I love you
❑ I care about you
❑ You are important
❑ You are awesome
❑ You deserve a treat
❑ I want to help you
❑ Other _____

This ticket entitles you to:

FROM:

TICKET

TICKET

TO:

Because:
❑ I love you
❑ I care about you
❑ You are important
❑ You are awesome
❑ You deserve a treat
❑ I want to help you
❑ Other _____

This ticket entitles you to:

FROM:

TICKET

TICKET

TO:

Because:
❑ I love you
❑ I care about you
❑ You are important
❑ You are awesome
❑ You deserve a treat
❑ I want to help you
❑ Other _____

This ticket entitles you to:

FROM:

TICKET

Interviewing Our Elders

Name

Birthday

Birth Place

Favorite Color

Favorite Animal

A Memory That Makes You Smile...

A Hope For The Future...

How I Can Pray For You...

Matching Game

Saying kind words	Sharing	Helping with a task	Cleaning my home
Reading to them	Singing a song	Playing a game	Giving a hug or a high five
Saying "thank you"	Creating art for them	Saying kind words	Sharing
Helping with a task	Cleaning my home	Reading to them	Singing a song
Playing a game	Giving a hug or a high five	Saying "thank you"	Creating art for them

6. Do Not Kill

Objectives

The children will:

- consider the negative and positive meanings of the sixth commandment,
- learn that God is a God of love and forgiveness,
- wonder how to respect the image of God in a person, and
- explore the role of the sixth commandment in keeping a community healthy and safe.

Bible Story

God creates everything and calls it good. (Genesis 1)

Bible Verse

Do not kill. (Exodus 20:13)

Focus for the Teacher

The sixth commandment not to kill is another seemingly straightforward commandment. What more is there to say? Do not kill. Of course, it is not that simple. What about situations of self-defense? What about stopping other violence? What about war? What about the death penalty? Already you can see that the sixth commandment is deeply complex.

Like the other commandments, there is a negative side and a positive side to this commandment. "Do not kill" is phrased in the negative. But what is the positive? For this, we look to today's Bible story in Genesis 1. God calls everything God created "good." With this, we can infer that God wants us to treat all of creation with respect, especially the human beings whom God created in God's own precious image.

Elsewhere in the Bible, the questions of violence in the case of self-defense and war are addressed. See chapter 6 in *Words of Life* for more information. However, the Bible offers some beautiful images of what a world without violence would be like, as in Isaiah 2:4: "Then they will beat their swords into iron plows / and their spears into pruning tools. / Nation will not take up sword against nation; / they will no longer learn how to make war." And Isaiah 11:

The wolf will live with the lamb,
  and the leopard will lie down with the
  young goat;

the calf and the young lion will feed together,
  and a little child will lead them.
The cow and the bear will graze.
  Their young will lie down together,
  and a lion will eat straw like an ox. . . .

They won't harm or destroy anywhere on my holy mountain.
  The earth will surely be filled with the knowledge
  of the LORD,
  just as the water covers the sea.

(Isaiah 11:6-7, 9a)

Addressing the sixth commandment with children requires care and grace. Some children may be disturbed by conversations about death, and some may have had family experiences with someone being killed. For these reasons, the main focus of the activities in this section is on treating human beings with respect and honoring the image of God in others. As you lead, focus on the "positive" side of the sixth commandment, treating others with respect and justice. Reinforce the goodness of all creation and God's overwhelming power and love. Explore the prophet's dreams for a world without sin, violence, and destruction. Keep an open mind and a sensitive heart while you lead this session, and God will be with you, working in the children's hearts.

Explore Interest Groups

Adult leaders should prepare the space before the children arrive. When children arrive, welcome them by name and invite them into the space. Briefly give them a choice of activities and set clear time boundaries. For children struggling with transitions, it can be helpful to have a timer set and be able to give an estimate of the length of time activities will take.

Respect Posters (Younger Children)

- **ASK:** How do you feel when people say nice words to you? When someone gives you a compliment? How does it feel when you say nice words to other people?

- **SAY:** I'm glad you know how to speak kindly to others and receive kind words back to you. But, sometimes people need a reminder to be kind to one another. Let's make some reminders that we can put around the church.

- Direct children to write on the pieces of paper "Respect the imago Dei" or "Respect God's image" and "Kind words spoken here."

- **ASK:** How do you hope people will feel when they see these posters? How do you hope people will act?

- Laminate the posters if desired and a laminator is accessible.

- Hang the posters in your church building where many people can see them.

Prepare

- ✓ **Supplies:** plain paper, markers, laminate sheets, and laminator (if desired)
- ✓ Make an example.

Image of God Mirror (Older Children)

- Give each child a photo frame and mirror paper. Have them glue the mirror paper onto the frame. Then direct them to decorate the frame.

- If you are using cosmetic mirrors, have them decorate using stickers and permanent markers around the edge of the mirror.

- Have each of them write "imago Dei" or "image of God" on the mirror.

- **ASK:** What do you see when you look in the mirror? How does it feel to see a reminder that you are made in the image of God when you look in the mirror?

- **SAY:** The image of God is all around us, a reminder that God created all of the world and all humans with love. We must respect the image of God wherever we find it, especially in one another.

Prepare

- ✓ **Supplies:** mirrors (small cosmetic mirrors or mirror paper), craft photo frames, markers, stickers, glue
- ✓ Make an example. If you have mirror paper, cut mirror paper to match the size of the photo frames.

Large Group (All Ages)

Bring all the children together to experience the Bible story. Ring jingle bells to alert the children to the large group time.

Prepare

✓ **Supplies:** posterboard, markers, Bible (*Deep Blue Kids*)

✓ Write the Bible verse on the posterboard.

Bible Story

- Invite the children to sit in a circle.

- **SAY:** Over the past few sessions we have been learning about the Ten Commandments and how they help us live in right relationship with God and in healthy and safe relationships with people. The first four commandments show us how to worship God. The last six commandments help us understand how to live in peace with other people. Today we are reading the sixth commandment.

- Have the children read the Bible verse from the poster aloud together.

- **SAY:** Our Bible verse today seems really simple. It's very direct. "Do not kill." Some people think it is mostly talking about not killing any person, even in a war or in self-defense. Some even take it more seriously and believe it means don't kill any animals or insects.

- **ASK:** What does this commandment mean to you?

- **SAY:** We know that the commandments always have two sides. We can understand that they tell us what we shouldn't do, but they also tell us what we should do.

- **ASK:** What do you think the opposite of killing is? What is the other side of the sixth commandment? How does this commandment want us to behave?

- Invite the children to listen as you read Genesis 1. If desired, have a strong reader assist you.

- **ASK:** Why did God call everything God created "good"? What does this tell us about how we should treat God's creation?

- **SAY:** Killing disrespects the image of God in someone. That is really serious. Instead we should have respect for the image of God and recognize that God loves all people.

- **ASK:** How does the sixth commandment help us live with healthy and safe relationships to our community?

Image of God

- **SAY:** Each of you is made in the image of God. All of creation is like God's self-portrait. Because each of you is made in God's image, you are special and loved. And all of us must treat other people with kindness.

- Give each child a sheet of paper. Have them each draw a self-portrait. At the top of each portrait, have each child write "I am made in the image of God."

- Encourage the children to write or draw what is special about each of them, and how they want to be treated.

- **ASK:** What is it like to treat someone with kindness? What is it like for someone to treat you with kindness?

Prepare

✓ **Supplies:** paper, markers, pencils, assorted art materials

✓ Make an example.

Flip Side

- Give each child a pencil and two sheets of cardstock (or one heart and one X cut out already).

- **SAY:** Each of the Ten Commandments has two sides. The way they are written in the Bible is often phrased as a "do not…" That makes me wonder, "What then should we do?" For the sixth commandment, "do not kill," the opposite is to respect God's image in other people.

- Direct each child to cut out a heart and an X shape from the cardstock. The X shape is the "do not" side of the commandment. The heart shape is the "do" side. Have them color the cardstock. Then use tape to fix the images back to back with the pencil in the middle.

- Have the children twirl the pencil back and forth in their hands to see both sides of the commandment.

Prepare

✓ **Supplies:** pencils, tape, cardstock, scissors, crayons, markers

✓ Make an example. If you are concerned about timing, cut out heart shapes and X shapes before class.

Small Groups

Divide the children into small groups. You may organize around age levels or around readers and nonreaders. Keep the groups small, with a maximum of ten children in each group. You may need to have more than one of each group.

Prepare

✓ **Supplies:** internet-connected device, plain paper, crayons, markers

✓ Load the image of John August Swanson's *Peaceable Kingdom* on your device. (Here is one address: https://www.eyekons.com/john_swanson_serigraphs/john_swanson_peaceable_kingdom_s)

Peaceable Kingdom (Younger Children)

- Look at the *Peaceable Kingdom* image. Invite children to name what they see in the image. If needed, prompt them with questions about colors and animals.

- **ASK:** This painting is called *Peaceable Kingdom*. It is an image that shows the world living in peace. What would your "peaceable kingdom" look like? Who would be there? What kinds of animals would be there?

- Give each child a plain piece of paper. Invite them to color what their "peaceable kingdom" looks like.

Prepare

✓ **Supplies:** plain or lined paper, pencils, crayons, markers

Hurting the Image of God (Older Children)

- **SAY:** God loves all people and has created all people in the image of God. We also know that even though we want to be kind to all people, sometimes we are mean instead. Sometimes we do or say unkind things that hurt the image of God.

- **ASK:** How does it feel when we do something that hurts the image of God in other people? Or when someone does something to us that hurts the image of God in us?

- Give each child a piece of paper. Invite the children to journal privately about any relationship they would like to repair. Give them five to ten minutes to do this.

- **SAY:** Part of how God loves us is that God forgives us when we don't do or say what we should. God loves us all the time, and gives us a second chance.

Closing Worship (All Ages)

Bring all the children back together into the large group for closing worship.

Ten Commandments Mobile

- Invite the children to share their artistic creations if desired.

- **SAY:** God gave us the Ten Commandments to show us how to live in a healthy and safe relationship with God and with people. Today we learned that God does not want us to cause harm to other people or other beings because that dishonors the image of God. Instead, we should respect the image of God in all people.

- Add the sixth commandment to the mobile by attaching it with string.

- **SAY:** Remember that the Ten Commandments are all about balance. They are guidelines for living so that we can have good relationships with God and with our community.

- **ASK:** How does not causing harm create a healthy community? How do you hope others will respect the image of God in you?

- **PRAY:** *Holy God, we give thanks for how you created everything with love. Help us know how to respect each of your wonderful creations and respect your image in every person. Amen.*

Prepare

✓ **Supplies:** sixth commandment cutout from Resource Page 1-4 from chapter 1, string, hole punch, Ten Commandments Mobile

✓ Cut out the sixth commandment from Resource Page 1-4 from chapter 1. Use a hole punch to create a hole and put string through it.

7. Faithfulness to God, Ourselves, and Others

Objectives

The children will:

- hear Psalm 139, about God's special love for creation, including humans;
- consider each person's uniqueness and importance to God;
- learn about respecting people's bodies and hearts; and
- explore healthy and safe relationships.

Bible Story

Psalm 139

Bible Verse

Do not commit adultery.
(Exodus 20:14)

Focus for the Teacher

Like the sixth commandment, the seventh commandment against adultery may seem like a lesson not well suited for children. And certainly, there are challenges to addressing this topic with children. The Bible story for the day, Psalm 139, can help guide the conversation. Psalm 139 affirms the individual worth of each person, body and identity. The "positive" side to the seventh commandment is that we should treat our bodies and hearts, and others' bodies and hearts, with respect. God's beautiful creation, spoken of poetically in Psalm 139, affirms the uniqueness and importance of each person.

When talking about bodies, consent is an important topic. In all your work with children, it is beneficial, for them and you, to respect people's boundaries when it comes to being touched. Try not to shame or guilt someone into giving a hug, holding hands, or for not doing those actions. Empower children to set their own boundaries for when they are touched and help them respect the boundaries others have. Phrases like "we don't touch people if they say 'no,'" "listen to what [NAME] is saying about her body," and "sometimes we don't feel like holding hands, and that's okay. Everyone has a choice!" may be helpful.

The seventh commandment against adultery is about healthy relationships among people, including emotional, physical, and sexual relationships. But another aspect is respecting one's own body. For this reason, part of the focus for this session is on affirming each person's body. When people affirm and respect their own bodies, they are more likely to affirm and respect others' bodies, too. And they will be more empowered to resist any temptation they have to say or act on desires they know are not healthy or safe.

Being a children's faith educator can be complicated, and intimidating, and this is one of those times that might seem especially difficult. Consider for yourself what your own boundaries are, with your body, your heart, and how you conduct yourself in relationships. You don't have to give details about your personal life to children, of course, but they will pick up on your attitude as a trusted adult. As you prepare to lead, be honest and welcome all questions that children may ask. Engage with children's parents or guardians, and with the pastor, if you hear anything that concerns you, or you sense a child may want to follow up on this topic. This may also be a good time to reinforce Safe Sanctuary rules within your congregation and children's ministries as well. With God's grace, you will be the leader the children need you to be as you affirm the inherent worth of each child.

Explore Interest Groups

Adult leaders should prepare the space before the children arrive. When children arrive, welcome them by name and invite them into the space. Briefly give them a choice of activities and set clear time boundaries. For children struggling with transitions, it can be helpful to have a timer set and be able to give an estimate of the length of time activities will take.

"I Like Me" (Younger Children)

- Give each child a copy of Resource Page 7-1.
- **SAY:** Every human being is a gift from God. It is important that we treat one another's bodies and hearts with respect and that we respect our own bodies and our own hearts.
- **ASK:** You can do amazing things with your bodies and your brains. What can you do that you are proud of?
- Have each child complete Resource Page 7-1.

Prepare

- ✓ **Supplies:** Resource Page 7-1, pencils
- ✓ Make copies of Resource Page 7-1.

Respect Collaborative Poster (All Ages)

- **SAY:** It is important to respect one another because we are all beautiful beings created by a loving God.
- **ASK:** How can you respect yourself? How can you treat your body kindly? How can you treat your heart kindly?
- **SAY:** As a promise that we will respect ourselves and respect others, let's paint this poster together.
- Have the children use finger paint to paint the poster.
- Let the poster dry. Hang it up in your space or in another location in your church.

Prepare

- ✓ **Supplies:** large posterboard or butcher paper, finger paint, permanent markers, paper cups
- ✓ Cover a table with plastic or a tablecloth to create a clean workspace. Draw the outlines of the word *RESPECT* on the butcher paper/posterboard. Fill paper cups with finger paint.

Good Bodies (All Ages)

- Give each child two pieces of watercolor paper. Have them trace their hands and feet with crayons. Direct them to write the word *good* in each handprint and footprint.
- Have children use watercolor paints to paint around their hands and feet.
- **SAY:** Our bodies are good. We should treat our bodies and others' bodies well, and also treat others' hearts and minds well.

Prepare

- ✓ **Supplies:** watercolor paper, watercolors, paintbrushes, crayons, cups, water
- ✓ Prepare a clean workspace using a tablecloth or plastic table covering.

Large Group (All Ages)

Bring all the children together to experience the Bible story. Ring jingle bells to alert the children to the large group time.

Prepare

✓ **Supplies:** posterboard, markers, Bible (*Deep Blue Kids*)

✓ Write the Bible verse on the posterboard.

Bible Verse

- Invite the children to sit in a circle.

- **SAY:** Over the past few sessions we have been learning about the Ten Commandments and how they help us live in right relationship with God and in healthy, safe relationships with people. The first four commandments show us how to worship God. The last six commandments help us understand how to live in peace with other people.

- Have the children read the Bible verse from the poster aloud together.

- **SAY:** This Scripture uses the word *adultery*. That's a big word that people today don't use a lot anymore. It means being reckless with your body and unfaithful in a marriage. Like other commandments, this commandment has two sides. The other side of this commandment is that God wants us to treat our bodies with respect and treat our relationships with others with kindness and justice.

Bible Story

- **SAY:** Our Bible verse today is from the Psalms. The Book of Psalms is a book of poetry in the Bible. The poetry expresses some of the biggest and most complicated emotions people can feel. The psalms also cry out to God and tell who God is and what God does for humanity. This psalm is one of the most famous ones, telling about how much God loves humans and cares for us.

- Invite the children to listen as you read Psalm 139.

- **ASK:** What does this psalm say about God creating humans? How does God know us and care for us?

- **SAY:** God loves us all the time. God knows our thoughts and our actions, and loves us always. Each human is created to be specially themselves.

Resisting Temptation

- **SAY:** Part of being human is making mistakes. Sometimes we really want to do something or say something when we know it's not right or good. This feeling is called *temptation*. Whenever we feel tempted to do or say something we know we shouldn't, these are some helpful things to remember.

- Give each child a copy of Resource Page 7-2 and a notecard.

- Have the children cut out the Five R statements. Direct them to glue the statements to a notecard.

- **SAY:** One of the Rs is to reveal your struggle to a trusted adult. If you are having a problem, are uncomfortable with how someone is treating you, or have questions about a situation, it is important to talk to an adult whom you trust.

- **ASK:** Who are trusted adults for you? (for example, family members, pastors, teachers, and so forth)

- **SAY:** Take your cards home so you can be reminded of the Five R statements in the weeks ahead.

Prepare

✓ **Supplies:** Resource Page 7-2, scissors, glue, 3" x 5" or larger notecards

✓ Make copies of Resource Page 7-2 and cut each copy in half, one for each child.

Web of Support

- **SAY:** Part of the seventh commandment is that God wants us to have healthy relationships. God wants us to work together instead of working against one another. We all have people who are kind of like partners in our lives, who help us grow and whom we trust.

- **ASK:** Who are your partners? Are they family? friends? teammates? friends from church?

- Give each child one paper plate and one length of yarn. Have them punch eight holes equally spaced around the ridged area of the plate, about 1½" from the edge.

- Direct the children to write the names of persons or draw images of the people they are in partnership with next to each of the holes.

- Have the children weave the yarn through all of the holes across the plate, making a web between all of the people.

- **SAY:** Whenever you see this web, remember that God wants us all to work together. Having partners we can work with can help make our communities strong.

Prepare

✓ **Supplies:** paper plates, hole punch, yarn, markers

✓ Cut yarn into 6' lengths. Make an example.

Small Groups

Divide the children into small groups. You may organize around age levels or around readers and nonreaders. Keep the groups small, with a maximum of ten children in each group. You may need to have more than one of each group.

Prepare

- ✓ **Supplies:** Resource Page 7-3, scissors, tape, cardstock
- ✓ Print Resource Page 7-3 on cardstock.

Heart Fan (Younger Children)

- **SAY:** God created each of us to be unique. God loves each of us all the time. We must each remember to treat our hearts well and treat others' hearts with kindness, because God first loved us.

- Give each child a copy of Resource Page 7-3. Have them color then cut out the hearts, leaving the hearts touching in the middle. Direct the children to fold the hearts on the dotted line. Tape the hearts together so they are back to back with "Psalm 139" facing outward.

Prepare

- ✓ **Supplies:** posterboard, markers, scissors, yarn, hole punch
- ✓ Draw bubble letters spelling LOVE on the posterboard, one set for each child, and cut them out.

Healthy Love Banner (Older Children)

- **SAY:** The seventh commandment tells us not to treat one another's bodies and hearts recklessly. Instead, we must try to have healthy relationships and love one another well.

- **ASK:** What does healthy love look like? What does it feel like? How do people act when they have a healthy and safe relationship?

- Give each child a set of the LOVE bubble letters. Invite them to write or draw to decorate the cutout letters.

- After the letters are decorated, have the children use the hole punch to string the letters together on the yarn.

Closing Worship (All Ages)

Bring all the children back together into the large group for closing worship.

Ten Commandments Mobile

- Invite the children to share their artistic creations if desired.

- **SAY:** God gave us the Ten Commandments to show us how to live in a healthy and safe relationship with God and with other people. Today we learned that God wants us to have healthy relationships with one another and treat one another's bodies and hearts with kindness and fairness.

- Add the seventh commandment to the mobile by attaching it with string.

- **SAY:** Remember that the Ten Commandments are all about balance. They are guidelines for living so that we can have good relationships with God and with our community.

- **ASK:** How does treating one another's bodies and hearts with respect help a community be strong? What can you do to help create healthy and safe relationships in your communities?

- **PRAY:** *Holy God, thank you for showing us how to love with justice and kindness. Help us create healthy relationships with our friends, families, and neighbors. Amen.*

Prepare

- ✓ **Supplies:** seventh commandment cut out from Resource Page 1-4 from chapter 1, string, hole punch, Ten Commandments Mobile

- ✓ Cut out the seventh commandment from Resource Page 1-4 from chapter 1. Use a hole punch to make a hole and put string through it.

I Like Me

 With my heart,

I can _____

 With my hands,

I can _____

 With my feet,

I can _____

 With my brain,

I can _____

 With my mouth,

I can _____

 With my joy,

I can _____

 With my prayer,

I can _____

Resisting Temptation

Remember who you are

Recognize consequences

Rededicate yourself to God

Reveal your struggle to a trusted adult.

Remove yourself from the temptation.

Resisting Temptation

Remember who you are

Recognize consequences

Rededicate yourself to God

Reveal your struggle to a trusted adult.

Remove yourself from the temptation.

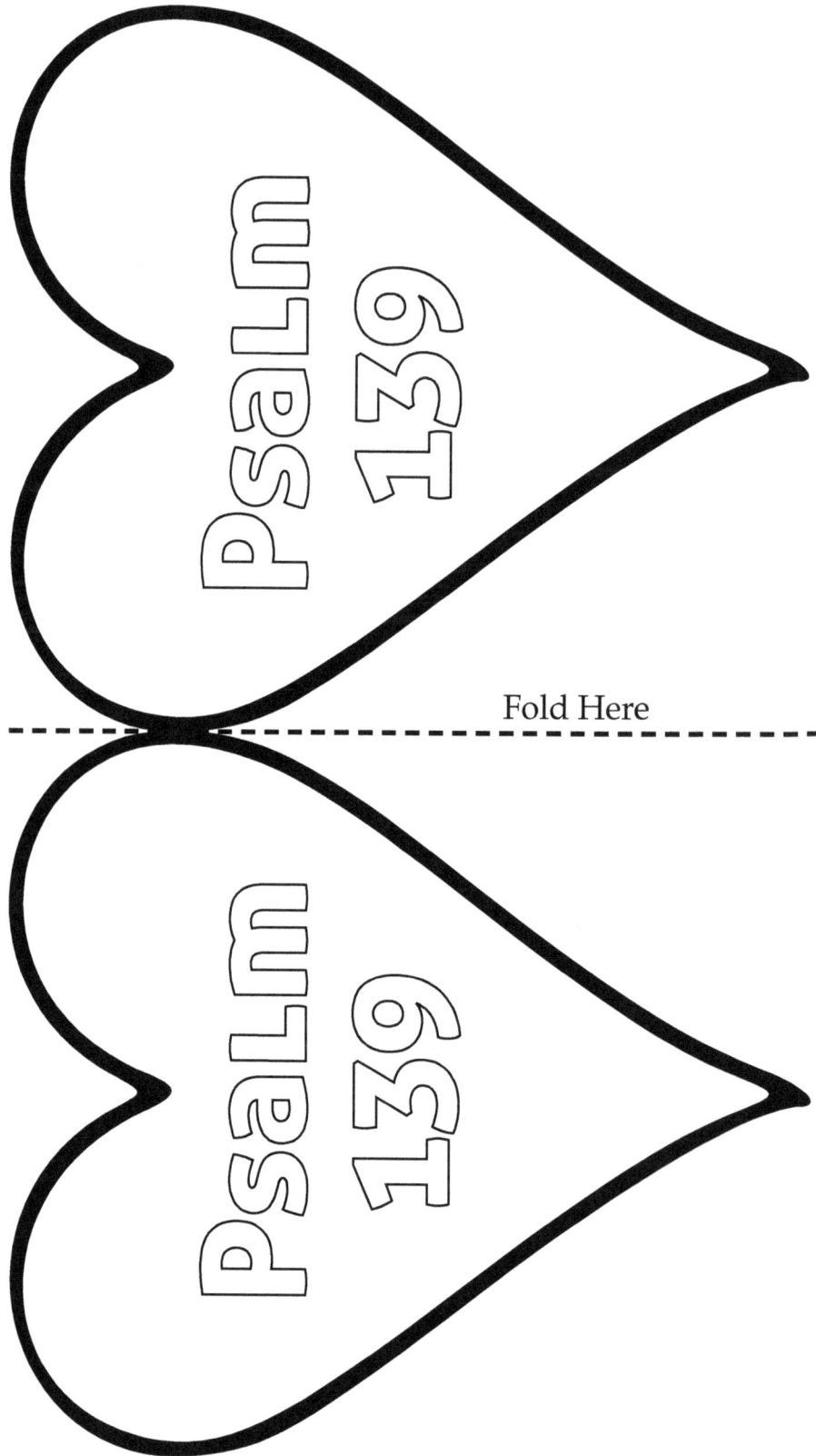

Heart Fan

Psalm 139

Fold Here

Psalm 139

8. Stealing Is Wrong

Objectives

The children will:

- hear about the prohibition for stealing,
- explore why stealing is wrong,
- learn that generosity is the opposite of stealing, and
- consider how to be generous by sharing skills through volunteering or sharing with the church through tithing.

Bible Story

Part of God's instructions to the Israelites, giving more details about how to follow the commandments and keep God's covenant.

(Exodus 22:1)

Bible Verse

Do not steal. (Exodus 20:15)

Focus for the Teacher

When I was ten, I saved my money to buy Elton John's *Greatest Hits* on vinyl. I rode my bike to the Jones Store, a large department store a couple of blocks from my home, and went straight to the record department to find the album. To my dismay, the price was $5.98. I'd thought it was $4.98....I was $1 short.

Instead of going home, I had a devious thought. Why not replace the price tag with one from another album that was at the lower price?...I carefully peeled a price tag from another album and placed it over the tag on the Elton John album. Then I carried it to the register and waited for a clerk to show up....The cashier finally arrived at the register and rang me up for $4.98. I walked out with my album and a lot of remorse.

Hamilton encourages us to take an honest look at how stealing has impacted our lives. The vast majority of us are not bank robbers or looters, but we still may be guilty of stealing. Maybe we seek out shopping deals even when we can afford the full price, contributing to less money going back to laborers. Maybe we are always late to meetings, as Hamilton describes, thus "stealing time" from the people we meet with. Maybe we let work trickle into our home lives, stealing time, space, or energy from our commitments to family and friends.

As with all of the commandments, the eighth commandment against stealing has a positive side. The "do" side of the eighth commandment focuses toward generosity. Instead of stealing, we must try to be generous to all we meet. This also goes for our involvement at church—tithing! How are we generous with our resources for the glory of God and the benefit of our church community? Jesus encourages generosity in his parables (see Matthew 25) and the Proverbs are full of quotable examples (see Proverbs 22).

Part of growing up is learning about the boundaries of ownership. Most children go through a phase where they learn what is theirs and what belongs to someone else. Most children are confronted with the opportunity to take something that is not theirs, perhaps encouraged by a playground dare or an honest desire for something they need. Today's Bible story in Exodus gives specific examples of the consequences of stealing, answering questions about how to repair the relationship between a thief and the owner of stolen items. As you lead, encourage the children to be honest about experiences they've had with stealing. Recognize socioeconomic differences among your group, as some children may be more concerned with protecting their material possessions than making sure everyone has basic needs met. And, the tithing exercise gives them an opportunity to experience an important aspect of supporting God's work through the faith community. Honesty and grace accompany lessons about generosity in this session.

Words of Life: Children's Leader Guide

Explore Interest Groups

Adult leaders should prepare the space before the children arrive. When children arrive, welcome them by name and invite them into the space. Briefly give them a choice of activities and set clear time boundaries. For children struggling with transitions, it can be helpful to have a timer set and be able to give an estimate of the length of time activities will take.

Map of Giving (Younger Children)

- Give each child a copy of Resource Page 8-1.

- Have them connect the dots to reveal the pathway.

- **ASK:** What pictures of giving do you see along this pathway? How do you give your (time, energy, helping, and so forth) in your life?

- Invite children to add their own drawings to the map of giving.

Prepare

- ✓ **Supplies:** Resource Page 8-1, crayons, markers

- ✓ Make copies of Resource Page 8-1.

Who Gives? (Older Children)

- Give each child a copy of Resource Page 8-2.

- Have them complete the word search. Then have them match up the found words with their descriptions at the bottom of the page.

- **ASK:** What do these people have in common? How do each of them help children? How do each of them help the community?

Prepare

- ✓ **Supplies:** Resource Page 8-2, pencils

- ✓ Make copies of Resource Page 8-2.

- ✓ *Answers:*
  BUS DRIVER
  COACH
  DOCTOR
  FIREMAN
  FRIEND
  MAYOR
  PARENT
  PASTOR
  TEACHER

ANSWER KEY:

B	R	O	T	C	O	D	T	S	K	P	K
K	U	S	M	T	A	E	P	F	M	T	D
D	B	S	V	A	A	U	R	I	H	Z	T
X	N	I	D	C	Y	O	X	R	J	T	X
V	Q	E	H	R	T	O	T	E	T	G	B
P	G	E	I	S	I	A	R	M	N	G	W
E	R	G	A	R	W	V	I	A	E	B	D
Y	I	P	W	N	F	I	E	N	R	J	C
V	R	B	D	T	D	D	R	R	A	W	S
Z	U	X	Q	D	U	S	C	I	P	R	B
H	L	R	B	J	D	D	Q	E	F	L	H
V	T	N	C	Q	C	O	A	C	H	E	I

Large Group (All Ages)

Bring all the children together to experience the Bible story. Ring jingle bells to alert the children to the large group time.

Prepare

✓ **Supplies:** posterboard, markers, Bible (*Deep Blue Kids*)

✓ Write the Bible verse on the posterboard.

Bible Verse

- Invite the children to sit in a circle.

- **SAY:** Over the past few sessions we have been learning about the Ten Commandments and how they help us live in right relationship with God and in healthy, safe relationships with people. The first four commandments show us how to worship God. The last six commandments help us understand how to live in peace with other people.

- Have the children read the Bible verse from the poster aloud together three times. Invite them to clap on each syllable.

- **ASK:** This seems like a pretty simple rule. What does it mean to not steal? Why shouldn't people steal? Is stealing always wrong?

- **SAY:** Our Bible story today takes place as part of a big speech that God makes to Moses. This is where God gives more details about the Ten Commandments and how they should be put into law.

Bible Story

- Invite the children to listen as you read Exodus 22:1.

- **ASK:** Why is it the rule that someone who steals something must give back more than they stole? Is it so anyone who might steal would be scared to do so? Or for another reason?

- **SAY:** Sometimes laws are made with consequences so that people will be convinced not to break them. That might be what is going on here. But this rule also shows us that generosity is the opposite of stealing, and generosity is more powerful.

- **ASK:** How are you generous? How do you share your talents or resources with others? Who is generous to you?

Tithing Exercise

- Give each child one cup holding fifty beans.

- **SAY:** The negative way to say the eighth commandment is to say "Do not steal." The positive idea that goes with it is "Be generous." One way that people are generous is by giving some of their resources to God's work in the world. This is called "tithing."

- **ASK:** When have you heard about "tithing"? Have you ever seen the church take an offering? Have you ever donated something?

- **SAY:** Tithing is like donating to the church. Many people try to give 10 percent of their resources as a tithe. Resources could be money, time volunteered, or things they have in their homes.

- Have the children dump the beans onto the floor in front of them. Direct the children to divide the beans into ten rows of five beans each.

- Using an empty cup, invite the children to take five of their beans (one whole row) and add them to your cup. Go around to each child and ask if they will give five of their beans.

- **SAY:** Each of us had fifty beans, and 10 percent of fifty is five. You can see how quickly all our beans add up in the cup when we are all contributing to one cup. When we all work together and are generous, we can make more happen than when we are just contributing on our own.

- **ASK:** What happens if some people have more beans? Or if some people have fewer beans?

- You may decide to do the exercise again, giving different people different amounts of beans. If so, continue to affirm that a larger group working together can accomplish more than individuals working separately.

Prepare

- ✓ **Supplies:** dried beans, paper cups

- ✓ Divide the beans into paper cups, one cup for each child. Put fifty beans in each cup.

Prepare

✓ **Supplies:** assorted art supplies, paper, cardboard boxes (used tissue boxes work well)

✓ Explore the community ministries your church is involved with. If possible, invite church members who are involved in these ministries or representatives from these ministries to visit your group and share about what they do.

Sharing Our Gifts

- **SAY:** The eighth commandment tells us that stealing is wrong. And we know the opposite of stealing is giving and being generous. Many churches have community partnerships with programs that help people. This is one way churches can be generous.

- Allow the visitors to your group to share. If you do not have visitors, **ASK:** What are some ministries this church is involved in? Have you ever volunteered your time?

- Invite the visitors to tell how the children can help them the most.

- Lead a discussion inviting the children to decide what community ministry to support and how to support the ministry.

- If your ministry involves collecting donated goods, divide children into groups of three or four. Distribute one cardboard box to each group. Invite them to decorate the boxes according to the work of the community ministry.

- As a large group, decide where in your church (or wider community) you will place these boxes.

Small Groups

Divide the children into small groups. You may organize around age levels or around readers and nonreaders. Keep the groups small, with a maximum of ten children in each group. You may need to have more than one of each group.

Giving Sign (Younger Children)

- Give each child one piece of posterboard and a copy of Resource Page 8-3. Have each child cut out the bubble letter words from Resource Page 8-3 and glue them to the posterboard.

- Have the children use paint to decorate the rest of the posterboard.

- As the paint dries, **SAY:** The opposite of stealing is giving. This sign can be a reminder for you and the people in your house that giving is important.

- **ASK:** Where do you think this sign will work best for your family?

Prepare

- ✓ **Supplies:** posterboard, paint, Resource Page 8-3, glue, scissors

- ✓ Make copies of Resource Page 8-3. Cover a table with a tablecloth or plastic to make a clean workspace. Cut each posterboard into three equal sections.

The Same Coin (Older Children)

- Give each child a plastic sandwich bag and a copy of Resource Page 8-4.

- **SAY:** We have learned that there are two sides to each commandment: a negative side that tells us what not to do and a positive side that tells us what we should do. Sometimes people use an expression that there are "two sides to the same coin." Today we are going to make coins with two sides that remind us of the eighth commandment. The negative side is the "do not steal" part, represented by money. The positive side is the "be generous" side, represented by the giving hands.

- Have each child color and cut out the coins. Then have them match up the money and the giving hands sides back to back and glue them.

- Store all of the coins in the sandwich bags.

Prepare

- ✓ **Supplies:** cardstock, Resource Page 8-4, glue, plastic sandwich bags or small fabric pouches, scissors, crayons

- ✓ Print Resource Page 8-4 on cardstock. Make some examples.

Closing Worship (All Ages)

Bring all the children back together into the large group for closing worship.

Prepare

✓ **Supplies:** eighth commandment cut out from Resource Page 1-4 from chapter 1, string, hole punch, Ten Commandments Mobile

✓ Cut out the eighth commandment from Resource Page 1-4 from chapter 1. Use a hole punch to create a hole and put string through it.

Ten Commandments Mobile

- Invite the children to share their artistic creations if desired.

- **SAY:** God gave us the Ten Commandments to show us how to live in a healthy and safe relationship with God and with other people. Today we learned that God does not want us to steal. We should not take what is not ours. The opposite of stealing is giving, and we should give generously.

- Add the eighth commandment to the mobile by attaching it with string.

- **SAY:** Remember that the Ten Commandments are all about balance. They are guidelines for living so that we can have good relationships with God and with our community.

- **ASK:** How does not stealing help a community be safe and healthy? What can you do to give generously to your community?

- **PRAY:** *Holy God, thank you for showing us how to give generously. Help us not want or feel the need to steal what is not ours. Instead, help us look for ways to be generous to all people. Amen.*

Map of Giving

School

Playground

Home

Church

Park

Grocery Store

Who Gives?

B	R	O	T	C	O	D	T	S	K	P	K
K	U	S	M	T	A	E	P	F	M	T	D
D	B	S	V	A	A	U	R	I	H	Z	T
X	N	I	D	C	Y	O	X	R	J	T	X
V	Q	E	H	R	T	O	T	E	T	G	B
P	G	E	I	S	I	A	R	M	N	G	W
E	R	G	A	R	W	V	I	A	E	B	D
Y	I	P	W	N	F	I	E	N	R	J	C
V	R	B	D	T	D	D	R	R	A	W	S
Z	U	X	Q	D	U	S	C	I	P	R	B
H	L	R	B	J	D	D	Q	E	F	L	H
V	T	N	C	Q	C	O	A	C	H	E	I

_____ This person helps students learn.

_____ This person preaches and teaches in the church.

_____ This is someone you can count on to listen, share, and play together.

_____ This person helps you grow.

_____ This person keeps the neighborhood safe from fire.

_____ This person teaches kids how to play sports.

_____ This person makes sure kids get to school safely and on time.

_____ This person helps the community stay healthy.

_____ This person helps make laws to keep the community safe.

Giving Sign

It Is Better To Give Than To Receive!

The Same Coin

9. The Power of Words

<table>
<tr><td>

Objectives

The children will:

- encounter stories about truth and lies in the Old and New Testaments,
- discover affirmations to encourage them when they are confronted with low self-esteem, and
- explore the challenge of discerning truth from lies.

</td><td>

Bible Story
Peter denies Jesus. (Luke 22:54-62)

Bible Verse
Do not testify falsely against your neighbor.

(Exodus 20:16)

</td></tr>
</table>

Focus for the Teacher

The ninth commandment can be confusing on the surface. What does a false testimony mean? That sounds like something for people in judicial situations. But false testimony has another common name: lying. Developmentally, children go through phases where they learn to tell the truth from lies and where they experiment with lying. Honesty is a good and important value to practice as you lead children through this session.

In ancient times there were, and in some places there still are, severe punishments for violating the ninth commandment. The USA is no different. Think of the importance of promising to tell "the whole truth and nothing but the truth" in court proceedings and the punishment for lying under oath. And in today's political world, it can be hard to tell truth from lies sometimes. If it is challenging for adults, think of how confusing it must be for children.

Discernment between truth and lies is important to develop. That's a big word for kids, so instead you can talk about how you know what is right and what is wrong, what is a lie and what is true. Discernment takes listening, and may be easier within a community who can help you listen and decide what actions are right and wrong.

One of the most insidious lies in society today is, sadly, encouraged by the prevalence of social media. This is the lie that we are worthless. From children to adults, social media can have a negative impact on self-esteem and self-image. Some people make it their work to cut others down, and children exposed to social media are far more vulnerable to these attacks than many like to admit. Because children in your group are probably still developing their sense of self, the focus of many activities in this session is on affirming each child's worth and importance. Another focus is on honesty and how to know what is right and wrong.

As a facilitator, you have a unique opportunity to affirm each child and shape how the conversations about honesty take place. By listening deeply, you encourage the children to listen deeply. By asking hard questions, you empower the children to do the same. You are ready for this task and this topic. God is with you.

Explore Interest Groups

Adult leaders should prepare the space before the children arrive. When children arrive, welcome them by name and invite them into the space. Briefly give them a choice of activities and set clear time boundaries. For children struggling with transitions, it can be helpful to have a timer set and be able to give an estimate of the length of time activities will take.

Connect the Dots (Younger Children)

- Give each child a copy of the Resource Page 9-1.

- Have them connect the dots.

- Help them read the Scripture verse.

Prepare

- ✓ **Supplies:** Resource Page 9-1, pencils

- ✓ Make copies of Resource Page 9-1.

Affirmation Sticks (All Ages)

- **SAY:** There are times in everyone's life when we need a reminder of who we are and why we are special. Sometimes people will say mean things to us or we will feel bad about ourselves and need a reminder that we are loved. In these times of low self-esteem, when we forget how important we are to God, it helps to have some nice words to say to ourselves.

- Give each child a bag of ten craft sticks. Have them choose some phrases from the example paper to write on the sticks.

- **ASK:** When might you use these sticks as a reminder that you are loved? Who else in your life might you want to share this activity with?

- Encourage the children to put their craft sticks back into their sandwich bags and look at them again any time they need a reminder they are loved.

Prepare

- ✓ **Supplies:** sandwich bags, permanent markers, wide craft sticks, and paper

- ✓ Write kind phrases on a paper as an example.

Large Group (All Ages)

Bring all the children together to experience the Bible story. Ring jingle bells to alert the children to the large group time.

Prepare

✓ **Supplies:** posterboard, markers, Bible (*Deep Blue Kids*)

✓ Write the Bible verse on the posterboard.

Bible Verse

- Invite the children to sit in a circle.

- **SAY:** Over the past few sessions we have been learning about the Ten Commandments and how they help us live in right relationship with God and healthy and safe relationships with people. The first four commandments show us how to worship God. The last six commandments help us understand how to live in peace with other people.

- Have the children read the Bible verse from the poster aloud together.

- **ASK:** What is a lie? Have you ever told a lie? Are some lies more serious than other lies?

Bible Story

- **SAY:** Today we have a Bible story that challenges us to think deeply about lying. The story is about what happened to Jesus's friends when Jesus was arrested.

- Invite the children to listen as you read Luke 22:54-62.

- **SAY:** Jesus told Peter before he was arrested that Peter would lie and say he didn't know Jesus. Peter didn't believe that he would ever do that! But the situation changed, and Peter was scared and lied.

- **ASK:** How do you think Peter felt when he lied about knowing Jesus? Why was it hard for him to tell the truth? How do you think Jesus felt when Peter lied about knowing him?

- **ASK:** Is it ever okay to lie? What about if someone is in danger and lying would protect that person?

Memory Truths and Lies

- Bring the tray into the middle of the circle. Allow the children to look at the tray for two minutes. Tell them to do their best to try to remember the items on the tray.

- Have the children split into pairs. Direct each child to think of two items that were on the tray and then make up another item. Have the partners tell each other which are the two true items and the one made-up item the other person identified.

- **ASK:** What was easy about this task? What was challenging? What was it like to figure out if your partner was telling the truth or making something up?

Telephone

- Have the children sit in a circle.

- **SAY:** Sometimes it is easy to listen and know what is true. Sometimes it is complicated. In our next game, listen closely to what your neighbor is saying.

- Start a game of "telephone" by whispering a tongue twister phrase in the ear of one of the children near you. Have each child repeat the phrase by whispering around the circle. When the last person has been told the phrase, have her or him share the phrase aloud to see if it is the same phrase that was whispered to the first child or a different one.

- Repeat the game if there is time.

- **SAY:** It can be easy to misunderstand what someone tells you. If you tell the truth and someone can misunderstand you, think of how much harder it would be to tell a lie and be misunderstood.

Prepare

✓ **Supplies:** cookie sheet, assorted small household objects, dishcloth or towel

✓ Arrange random small household objects on the cookie tray and cover it with a towel.

Small Groups

Divide the children into small groups. You may organize around age levels or around readers and nonreaders. Keep the groups small, with a maximum of ten children in each group. You may need to have more than one of each group.

Listen Closely (Younger Children)

- Invite children to stand in a circle.

- **SAY:** It can be hard to understand the differences between truth and lies sometimes. A good first step is listening closely.

- **ASK:** What does it take to be a good listener?

- Play a game of "Simon Says" with the kids. Invite them to close their eyes (if they are comfortable). Play for about three minutes.

- **ASK:** What was it like to play Simon Says with your eyes closed? What made it more challenging to listen? What would make it easier to listen?

Two Truths and a Lie (Older Children)

- **SAY:** Sometimes it is hard to tell truth from lies. Sometimes lies sound like the truth, and sometimes the truth can sound like lies. When we work together, it is easier to tell what is true and what is a lie.

- Have children sit in a circle.

- Pick one child to go first. Have that child think to himself or herself two true statements about himself or herself and then make up one lie. Have that child tell the whole group.

- Facilitate a conversation with the rest of the group to decide what are the true statements and what is a lie.

- Repeat this game with all the children who want to play.

- **ASK:** How do you tell what is true and what is a lie? What kinds of experiences do you think of when you are trying to decide between truth and lies?

Closing Worship (All Ages)

Bring all the children back together into the large group for closing worship.

Ten Commandments Mobile

- Invite the children to share their artistic creations if desired.

- **SAY:** God gave us the Ten Commandments to show us how to live in a healthy and safe relationship with God and with other people. Today we learned that God does not want us to lie to anyone, even ourselves. Instead, we should tell the truth and practice honesty.

- Add the ninth commandment to the mobile by attaching it with string.

- **SAY:** Remember that the Ten Commandments are all about balance. They are guidelines for living so that we can have good relationships with God and with our community.

- **ASK:** How does not telling lies help create a healthy and safe community? How does telling the truth affect a community?

- **PRAY:** *Holy God, we give thanks for the truth that you love us all the time. Help us practice honesty in our lives so that we can tell the truth about who we are and who you are to the world. Amen.*

Prepare

✓ **Supplies:** ninth commandment cut out from Resource Page 1-4 from chapter 1, string, hole punch, Ten Commandments Mobile

✓ Cut out the ninth commandment from Resource Page 1-4 from chapter 1. Use a hole punch to make a hole and put string through it.

Connect the Dots
Ephesians 4:29

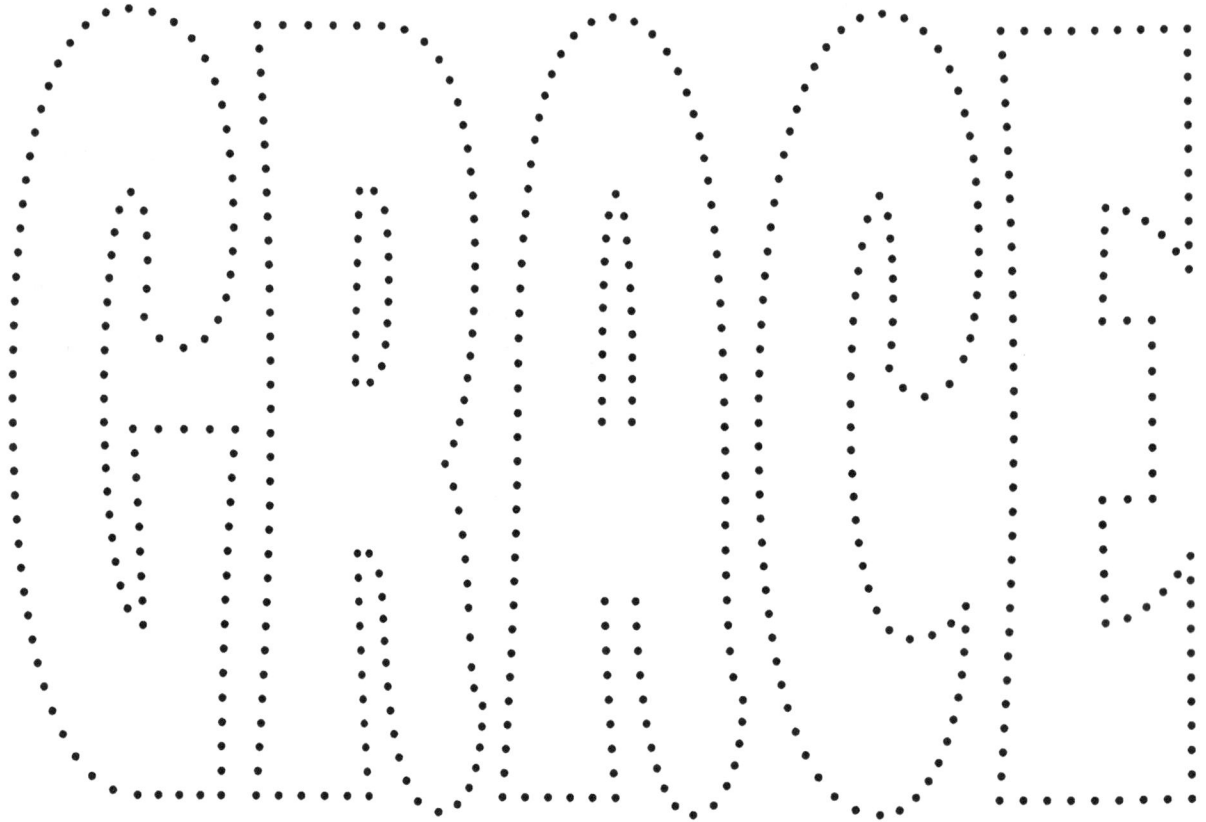

GRACE

Don't let any foul words come out of your mouth. Only say what is helpful when it is needed for building up the community so that it benefits those who hear what you say.

10. Wanting What Is Not Yours

Objectives

The children will:

- hear the story of Adam and Eve eating from the tree of the knowledge of good and evil,
- discover what it means to covet,
- explore how gratitude is the opposite of coveting, and
- learn what it means to be content with what you have.

Bible Story

Adam and Eve want God's knowledge and ignore God's rules. (Genesis 3:1-19)

Bible Verse

Do not desire and try to take your neighbor's house. Do not desire and try to take your neighbor's wife, male or female servant, ox, donkey, or anything else that belongs to your neighbor. (Exodus 20:17)

Focus for the Teacher

Here we are, the tenth commandment! Hopefully you have had enlightening and empowering conversations with the children in your group over the past several sessions. The tenth commandment may seem like a rather weak ending to the important topics addressed in the first nine commandments. But here's what Adam Hamilton says about the importance of the tenth commandment as a bookend with the first commandment:

> The first commandment and the tenth form a bracket: Both deal with the human heart, but from different angles. In the first commandment, we're told to have no other gods before God. The last commandment deals directly with those "other gods" humans have always tended to worship—the material possessions and even people we are prone to covet. In many ways coveting is often the motivation behind our violation of all of the commandments. Coveting can be a form of idolatry. It can lead us to misuse God's name or work on the Sabbath or dishonor our parents. It is sometimes behind the violence we do to one another and is, by definition, central to adultery and stealing—in both of these last two commandments, coveting leads us to take what is not ours. In a sense, even bearing false witness can be the result of a heart that craves attention or vengeance or a host of other things that can lead us to hurt others by falsely testifying about them.

Over the past several sessions, you probably touched on topics of jealousy, lying, temptation, living well, social justice, and individual self-esteem as you sought to understand the commandments and share their relevance with the children in your care. Coveting, as Adam Hamilton says, does address a lot of these aspects. The desire for something that is not yours has the flip side of "contentment." We might say that the "positive" side of the tenth commandment is to "be content." Gratitude is part of contentment and you can encourage the children to practice giving thanks for what they do have in their lives.

Do you practice gratitude in your own life? Again, you are an example of a caring and trusted leader for these children, and you have the power to set a good example. As you lead, encourage the children to practice gratitude. You can even make a point of saying "thank you" to children during the session and pointing out that "thank you" is an expression of gratitude. As you prepare for this session, know that the children in your group are grateful for you and your time and energy, as are their families and the rest of your community of faith. May this experience of leading children through encountering the Ten Commandments turn your heart toward gratitude to the Great Giver of All Things.

Explore Interest Groups

Adult leaders should prepare the space before the children arrive. When children arrive, welcome them by name and invite them into the space. Briefly give them a choice of activities and set clear time boundaries. For children struggling with transitions, it can be helpful to have a timer set and be able to give an estimate of the length of time activities will take.

Gratitude Journal (Older Children)

- Give each child four sheets of paper and one sheet of construction paper. Have them fold all of the papers in half ("hamburger" style). Nest the plain paper inside the construction paper like a book.

- Use a hole punch to make a hole about 2½" from the top of the fold and 2½" from the bottom of the fold. Have the children string yarn through the holes and tie the knot on the inside of the journal.

- Direct the children to draw a horizontal line on each page, splitting the page into a top half and bottom half. On the top half, write "Morning" and on the bottom half, write "Evening."

- **SAY:** One of the guidelines that God wants us to live by is being grateful. God doesn't want us to be jealous or always be wanting more, more, more. God wants us to treat every day with gratitude. That can be hard sometimes, and that's okay. The important thing is that we try to be grateful every day. So each day this week, try to write or draw something you are grateful for in the morning and in the evening.

Prepare

- ✓ **Supplies:** plain 8½" × 11" paper, construction paper, yarn, hole punch, markers, crayons
- ✓ Make an example.

Contentment Bracelet (All Ages)

- **SAY:** Sometimes we need reminders of how God wants us to live. Some people wear necklaces, bracelets, or T-shirts with special words on them to help them remember God's guidelines for living safe and healthy lives. Today we will make bracelets (or necklaces) that remind us to "be content" and not be jealous or envious of what someone else has.

- Help children cut lengths of string to fit their wrists.

- Have children thread beads onto their string. Include letter beads to spell the words "Be content" or the Scripture citation for the Bible verse for the day "Exodus 20:17."

Prepare

- ✓ **Supplies:** elastic string, scissors, pony beads, letter beads
- ✓ Make an example.

Prepare

✓ **Supplies:** thick yarn or ribbon, cardstock, scissors, hole punch, crayons, markers.

✓ Gather the supplies. Make an example.

Garland (All Ages)

- **SAY:** As we have learned that there are two sides to every commandment (a "do not" side and a "do" side), there is also one for the commandment we will learn about today. This commandment is number ten: do not covet. That means that we should not be jealous and want something we don't have, or something that shouldn't be ours. The other side of that commandment is: do be grateful. So we are going to make a garland to put up in our classroom or in our homes so we can remember to be grateful.

- Give each child five sheets of cardstock. Have them draw the letters of the word *GRATITUDE* in large bubble letters on the cardstock, two to a page. (One letter will be on a sheet of cardstock by itself.) Then have them use scissors to cut out the letters.

- Direct the children to use a hole punch to make holes and then string the letters onto the ribbon or yarn.

- Encourage the children to write or draw what they are grateful for on these letters.

- **ASK:** Where do you want to hang this garland? How will this be a reminder to you to be grateful?

Large Group (All Ages)

Bring all the children together to experience the Bible story. Ring jingle bells to alert the children to the large group time.

Bible Verse

- **SAY:** Over the past few sessions, we have been learning about the Ten Commandments. Remember that these commandments are God's guidelines to help humans live in right relationship with God and healthy and safe relationships with other people.

- **ASK:** What commandment do you think is the easiest one to follow? What commandment do you think is the hardest one to follow? Why?

- Invite the children to read the Bible verse aloud with you. Have the children read the verse "popcorn" style, where each child says only one word. After all the children have participated in saying one word of the verse, read it aloud again as a large group, loud and strong.

Bible Story

- Invite the children to listen as you read Genesis 3:1-19 aloud. Have them reflect the emotions of the story on their faces as you read.

- **ASK:** Have you ever wanted something someone else had? Or has someone else wanted what you have? What did you do? How did you deal with that situation?

- **SAY:** Adam and Eve wanted the wisdom and power that God had. That's why they disobeyed God's rule not to eat from the tree in the center of the garden of Eden. They wanted to be like God, or maybe even be as powerful as God.

- **ASK:** How did God react when God found out about Adam and Eve eating the fruit? What was the role of the serpent in the story?

- **SAY:** The tenth commandment is the last one. It kind of sums up all of the other ones. God doesn't want us to spend our whole lives wanting more things or to be someone we are not. God wants us to be content, and be grateful for what we have. But we also know that sometimes we don't have what we need to live healthy lives. Even in these kinds of times, we can practice being grateful, knowing God is with us and will never let us go.

Prepare

✓ **Supplies:** Bible (*Deep Blue Kids*), posterboard, markers

✓ Write the Bible verse on the posterboard.

Prepare

✓ **Supplies:** two different-colored tennis balls or handheld beanbag.

Commandment Ten

- Have the children sit on the floor in a circle.

- Tell a story about a time you had to share.

- As you ask the following questions, pass one of the items from one person to another around the circle.

- **ASK:** What is sharing? How do you share with someone? How do you ask if someone would share with you? Is it challenging to share?

- Introduce the second item to the circle. Describe that one of the items is "safe" and the other item is "out." You will pass the items around the circle at the same time, but in different directions. When you call "Commandment Ten" the children have to pause passing the items around the circle and whoever has an item to hold on to it. The person holding the "safe" item and the two people on either side of that person are "safe." The person holding the "out" item and the two people on either side of that person are "out" of the game. Then they become observers of the game.

- Play this game a few times.

- **ASK:** Where did you want to be sitting when there was just one item passed around? Where did you want to be sitting when there were two items? Where was the best place to be? Who was this game the easiest for?

- Ask the people who observed the game to share anything they observed.

- **SAY:** As we played this game, I noticed that some of you really wanted to be holding the "safe" item. Or to be next to the person holding the "safe" item. And, some others really did not want to be near the "out" item. Some people passed the safe item very slowly, hoping they could hold on to it. Other people passed the "out" item really fast, hoping to get rid of it! This reminds me of when someone is "coveting" something else. They have to deal with wanting it and then have to figure out how they will behave. God knows that none of us is perfect, and we all have things we want. But the important thing is how we behave when we want something. Will we choose to be jealous? Or choose to be grateful for what we do have?

Being Generous with My Church

- Give each child a copy of Resource Page 10-1.

- **SAY:** Instead of coveting what we don't have, God wants us to be grateful for what we do have. And when we are grateful, we often find ways to give to others. One example of this is when we take an "offering" in church. Everyone in church thinks about what they can give to the church. Some people give money, some people give their time, some people serve food or work with a community service program.

- **ASK:** How can you give to the church? What part of the church's life together do you want to contribute to?

- Help them complete the prompt.

- Encourage the children to take their copy of Resource Page 10-1 to the worship service and add it to the offering.

✓ **Supplies:** Resource Page 10-1, pencils, markers, crayons

✓ Make copies of Resource Page 10-1 and cut them in half.

✓ **TIP:** Work with the worship planning committee or pastoral staff to include children in collecting the offering.

Small Groups

Divide the children into small groups. You may organize around age levels or around readers and nonreaders. Keep the groups small, with a maximum of ten children in each group. You may need to have more than one of each group.

Prepare

✓ **Supplies:** tissue paper, scissors, hole punches, envelopes, markers, crayons, tape

✓ Make an example.

✓ **TIP:** You can also use dried leaves or flower petals for confetti!

Prepare

✓ **Supplies:** Resource Page 10-2, pencils, markers, crayons

✓ Make copies of Resource Page 10-2.

Spreading Joy (Younger Children)

• **SAY:** The opposite of "coveting" is being grateful for what you have. Practicing gratitude each day can help you feel more joyful and want to share it with others.

• Direct children to pick several colors of tissue paper. Give each child an envelope. Use either a hole punch or scissors, or both, to cut tissue paper into small pieces of confetti. Encourage the children to put the confetti in their envelopes right away to decrease the mess.

• On the envelopes, help the children write the name of someone they are grateful for. Have the children decorate the envelope to say "I'm grateful for you!"

• **ASK:** How does gratitude help us share joy? How do you hope the person who receives this will feel?

• Encourage the children to give their envelope to someone they are grateful for.

Practicing Gratitude (Older Children)

• Give each child a copy of Resource Page 10-2.

• **ASK:** How does gratitude help us live according to the tenth commandment? How does gratitude help people live in a healthy and safe community?

• Invite the children to write or draw what they are grateful for in the spaces provided on Resource Page 10-2.

Closing Worship (All Ages)

Bring all the children back together into the large group for closing worship.

Ten Commandments Mobile

- Invite the children to share their artistic creations if desired.
- **SAY:** God gave us the Ten Commandments to show us how to live in a healthy and safe relationship with God and with other people. Today we learned that God doesn't want us to be jealous of what other people have. Instead, we should try to be content with what we do have and practice gratitude.
- Add the tenth commandment to the mobile by attaching it with string.
- **SAY:** Remember that the Ten Commandments are all about balance. They are guidelines for living so that we can have good relationships with God and with our community.
- **ASK:** How does being content with what you have help you live in a healthy community? How does gratitude help a community?
- **PRAY:** *Holy God, thank you for giving us what we need. We pray that we can help all people have what they need so no one will feel jealous or envious. Show us how to be grateful in every part of our lives. Amen.*

Prepare

- ✓ **Supplies:** tenth commandment cut out from Resource Page 1-4 from chapter 1, string, hole punch, Ten Commandments Mobile
- ✓ Cut out the tenth commandment from Resource Page 1-4 from chapter 1. Use a hole punch to put string through it.

Being Generous with My Church

I can give….

_____

_____

_____

_____

Being Generous with My Church

I can give….

_____

_____

_____

_____

Practicing Gratitude

I am grateful for what I have.		
People			
Places			
Things			
Feelings			

www.ingramcontent.com/pod-product-compliance
Lightning Source LLC
Chambersburg PA
CBHW080608090426
42735CB00017B/3372